Egyptian Colloquial Arabic Verbs

Exercise Book

Matthew Aldrich

lingualism

ISBN-10: 0985816015

ISBN-13: 978-0-9858160-1-8

website: www.lingualism.com

email: contact@lingualism.com

Contents

How To Use This Book

This exercise book is meant to be used in conjunction with Egyptian Colloquial Arabic Verbs: Conjugation Tables and Grammar (ISBN-10: 0985816007). Unless specifically mentioned, page numbers throughout this book refer to pages in Egyptian Colloquial Arabic Verbs: Conjugation Tables and Grammar, to which the reader is referred in order to complete the exercises.

Egyptian Colloquial Arabic Verbs: Exercise Book will provide you with ample practice to achieve accuracy and fluency in verb conjugation. The exercises have been designed to guide you through the rules of conjugation step-by-step, starting with the very basics of ECA verbs. **Absolute beginners** will find the exercises challenging and engaging. **More advanced learners** will find the first parts of the book a good review or refresher and will, in the latter parts, be able to pinpoint weaknesses in their conjugation skills and knowledge.

This exercise book is **not** meant to be a stand-alone course book. The focus of the exercise book is the morphology (formation) of Arabic verb conjugation. It is meant to provide supplementary exercises to learners so that they can improve accuracy and fluency in Egyptian Colloquial Arabic's seemingly complex system of verb conjugation. Learners will come to see that verb conjugation is actually quite straightforward and simple. It is, in fact, much more regular than English verb conjugation. With a few exceptions, the exercises in this book focus on the verb alone, and not in the context of complete sentences. The advantage here is that learners can focus on the formation of the verb itself, its prefixes, suffixes, and sound changes, without the added difficulty of having to deal with sentence grammar and vocabulary.

The exercises are meant to be done in order, starting with Part 1. If you are not an absolute beginner, and the first exercises seem "too" easy, it is best to work through them quickly rather than skip them altogether. One reason for this is that several skills, i.e. ways to look at verbs and rules for conjugation in general, are covered early on. In later parts of the book, you will continue to apply these skills and rules. In addition, the most common and useful verbs have been chosen to appear in the exercises. Learners are taught, or asked to find the meaning of, verbs when they *first* appear. In subsequent exercises, they will continue to appear, and it is expected that learners already know them.

A careful combination of variety in exercises coupled with repeated exercise types will help learners to start thinking more analytically about verb conjugation. In the first parts of the book, learners will receive careful directions as to what they should look for on which conjugation table, index, or appendix in order to find the information they need. In later parts, however, they will be expected to know what kind of information they need and how to find it in order to complete the exercises. This fosters independent learning.

The purpose of the exercises is to help you master verb conjugation, obviously. However, mastery cannot be achieved through completion of the exercises alone. Learners must continue to do drills. Techniques and resources for this are introduced at the end of part 2, and are found in the appendixes in the back of this book.

Feedback from learners is important for us to continue to improve the quality of our books. Please visit www.lingualism.com and let us know what you think.

Part 1: Sound Measure I Verbs

Section 1: The Pronouns

> Before we can begin conjugating verbs, we need to become familiar with the eight persons of Egyptian Colloquial Arabic (ECA), as each person has its own conjugation patterns.

1. Match each pronoun to its translation and description.

ána   híyya   húmma   íḥna   ínta   húwwa   íntu   ínti

1. _Ana_	I	first-person masculine/feminine singular
2. _Ihna_	we	first-person masculine/feminine dual/plural
3. _Inta_	you (m.)	second-person masculine singular
4. _Inti_	you (f.)	second-person feminine singular
5. _Intu_	you (pl.)	second-person masculine/feminine dual/plural
6. _Huwwa_	he; it (m.)	third-person masculine singular
7. _Hiyya_	she; it (f.)	third-person feminine singular
8. _Humma_	they	third-person masculine/feminine dual/plural

Section 2: The Base Form

> Compare the following forms of an English verb: *play, plays, played, playing.* The first is the base form, also called the citation form. It is the most basic form of a verb, as it has no affixes (prefixes or suffixes). The other forms are declined; that is, they have suffixes (*-s, -ed, -ing*).

1. Look at verb table 1s2 to answer the following questions.

1. Can you spot the most basic form of the verb, the base form? What is it?
2. Which person and tense is it?

2. Label the parts of the base form.

root	vowel of second syllable	second radical
vowel of first syllable	first radical	third radical

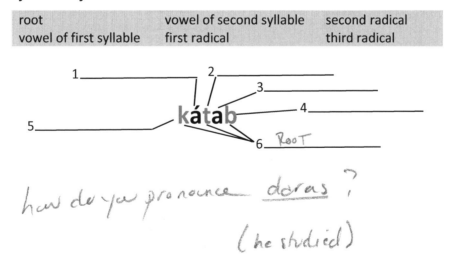

how do you pronounce *daras* ?

(he studied)

In section 1, we'll be looking at sound measure I verbs. Like **kátab**, all sound measure I verbs have three consonants. Notice that these consonants are gray in the tables and be changed out for consonants from other roots to conjugate other verbs. The base form, as we deduced in exercise 1, is the **húwwa** form of the perfect tense. While **kátab** can translate as *he wrote* when used as the verb in a sentence, it simply translates as its base form equivalent in English when cited: **kátab** means *write*. Keep in mind, also, that **húwwa** refers not only to a male human or animal, but any inanimate noun which is masculine according to Arabic grammar. **húwwa** can therefore also be translated as *it* in English.

3. Use the Verb Index by English Translation (p. 172 Note: Throughout this book, page numbers refer to Egyptian Colloquial Arabic Verbs: Congjugation Tables and Grammar) to translate the following. Remember that the cited form is the húwwa form of the perfect tense, so there is no need to conjugate.

1. he sent   *baɣat*
2. he attended   *hadar*
3. it arrived   *wasal*
4. he studied   *daras*
5. he did   *ɛamal*

6. he danced   *raʔas*
7. he requested   *talab*
8. he exited   *xarag*
9. it healed   *laham*
10. it was useful *nafaɛ*

Section 3: The Positive Perfect Tense

1. Change the following húwwa verbs into híyya verbs using tables 1s1-3.

1. kátab   *Katabit*
2. ṭálab   *talabit*
3. 3ámal   *ʒamalat*

4. ḍárab   *darabit*
5. náfa3   *nafa3it*
6. fátaħ   *fatahit*

Like **húwwa**, **híyya** can refer to an inanimate object and translate *it*, but it can also refer to the inanimate plural and translates *they*. However, to avoid ambiguity, in this exercise book **híyya** will always refer to a singular, and *they* will refer to **húmma**.

2. Translate your answers from exercise 1 into English.

1. ....
2. ....

3. ....
4. ....

5. ....
6. ....

3. Change the verbs from exercise 1 into húmma verbs using tables 1s1-3.

1. ....
2. ....

3. ....
4. ....

5. ....
6. ....

4. Crossword Puzzle: Use the Verb Index by English Translation on p. 172 to translate the following. Do not write in stress markers in the crossword.

across:
3. they described
5. they thanked
7. she paid
9. she guarded
10. he shaved

down:
1. she pronounced
2. they burned
4. she calculated
6. he researched
8. he stole

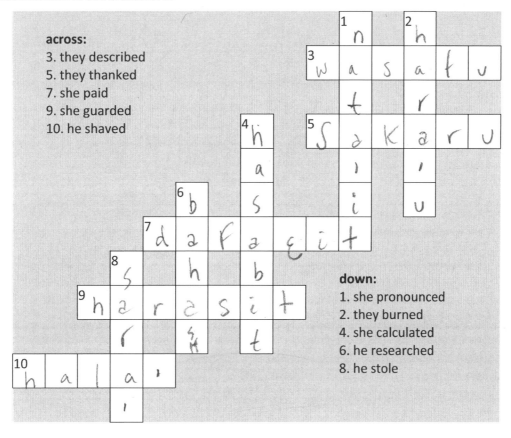

5. Change the following húwwa verbs into ínta verbs using tables 1s1-3 and translate. Notice the shift in stress, and be sure to mark the stressed syllable.

1. kátab ....Katabt.......
2. ṭálab ....talabt.......
3. ḍárab ....darabt.......

4. ʃákar ....ʃakart.......
5. xárag ....xaragt.......
6. wáṣaf ....wasaft.......
   'describe

6. Change the verbs from exercise 5 into ínti verbs using tables 1s1-3.

1. ...Katabti...
2. ...talabti...
3. ...darabti...
4. ...she karti...
5. ...Xaragti...
6. ...wasafti...

7. Change the verbs from exercise 5 into íntu verbs using tables 1s1-3.

1. ...Katabtu...
2. ...talabtu...
3. ...darabtu...
4. ...She kartu...
5. ...Xaragtu...
6. ...wasaftu...

8. Translate the following as if you were speaking to one man, one woman, and a group of people.

9 Egyptian Colloquial Arabic Verbs Exercise Book

	m	f	pl
1. you wrote	Katabt	Katabti	Katabtu
2. you exited	Xaragt	xaragti	xaragtu
3. you calculated	hasabt	hasabti	hasabtu
4. you studied	darast	darasti	darastu
5. you did	3amelt	3amelti	3ameltu

9. Translate the following.

1. he collected ....
2. she drew ....
3. they sat ....
4. you (m.) cooked ....
5. you (f.) weighed ....

6. you (pl.) broke ....
7. they washed ....
8. she touched ....
9. you (m.) parked ....
10. he entered ....

10. Change the following húwwa verbs into ána verbs using tables 1s1-3 and translate.

1. rásam ....
2. ṭálab ....
3. 3ámal ....

4. kátab ....
5. wázan ....
6. gáma3 ....

11. Change the verbs from exercise 10 into íḥna verbs using tables 1s1-3 and translate.

1. ....
2. ....
3. ....

4. ....
5. ....
6. ....

12. Translate the following.

1. I pronounced ....
2. we sat ....
3. you (m.) did ....
4. you (f.) touched ....

5. you (pl.) requested ....
6. he broke ....
7. she washed ....
8. they cooked ....

13. Complete the following verb tables.

	explained	spent	swept
ána			
íḥna			
ínta			
ínti			
íntu			
húwwa	ʃáraḥ	ṣáraf	kánas
híyya			
húmma			

14. Circle the words to complete the following sentences.

ECA has (1. three / eight / thirteen) persons. The (2. ána / húwwa) form is the base verb and takes no suffix. Other persons take a suffix. The suffixes for the (3. ána / ínti / híyya) and the (4. íḥna / íntu / húmma) forms start with a vowel, and so the word's stress (5. remains on the first syllable / shifts to the second syllable). The first- and second-person suffixes all begin with a (6. consonant / vowel), which causes the word's stress to (7.

shift to the second syllable / shift to the final syllable). The suffixes for the (8. ána / íŋna / húwwa) and (9. ínta / ínti / híyya) forms are identical but can be differentiated from the context of a sentence.

15. Use the Verb Index by Table for tables 1s4-6 (p. 124-125) to translate the following.

1. fíhim	....	5. líbis	....
2. sími3	....	6. misíktu	....
3. ʃiríbt	....	7. sikínti	....
4. 3irífna	....	8. lí3bit	....

16. Look at the positive perfect verbs in verb tables 1s4-6 to answer the following questions.

1. A vowel elides (drops), reducing a verb's syllable count, in certain persons. In which persons does this occur?
2. What are the vowels which elide?

17. Translate the following.

1. fíhmit	....	3. líbsu	....
2. sím3it	....	4. mísku	....

18. Translate the following.

1. I understood	....	6. we got dressed	....
2. they heard	....	7. she caught	....
3. she drank	....	8. they got dressed	....
4. you (f.) knew	....	9. she knew	....
5. you (pl.) drank	....	10. you (m.) understood	....

19. Use the Verb Index by English Translation (p. 172) to translate the following.

1. he laughed	....	6. you (f.) rode	....
2. she failed	....	7. they sneezed	....
3. they dreamed	....	8. I descended	....
4. you (m.) aged	....	9. she gave birth	....
5. they played	....	10. we shut up	....

20. Translate the following.

1. I studied	....	7. she shaved	....
2. misíkti	....	8. darástu	....
3. you (f.) pronounced	....	9. they understood	....
4. ʃiríbt	....	10. 3ámalit	....
5. he broke	....	11. you (m.) paid	....
6. simí3na	....	12. 3íṭis	....
13. we washed	....	17. she dreamed	....
14. lí3bit	....	18. ḫásabu	....
15. you (pl.) touched	....	19. they stole	....
16. ʔa3ádtu	....	20. wázan	....

Section 4: The Negative Perfect Tense

1. Look at verb tables 1s1-6. Make the following verbs negative and then translate.

1. kátab .... 4. fíhim ....
2. ṭálab .... 5. sími3 ....
3. ḍárab .... 6. líbis ....

2. Put the verbs from exercise 1 into the negative híyya form and then translate.

1. .... 4. ....
2. .... 5. ....
3. .... 6. ....

3. Put the following verbs into the negative form and then translate.

1. ṭálabu .... 3. sím3u ....
2. ḍárabu .... 4. líbsu ....

4. Translate the following verbs.

1. I didn't study .... 3. I didn't understand ....
2. I didn't work .... 4. you (m.) didn't understand ....

5. Translate the following verbs.

1. you (m.) didn't park .... 6. you (m.) didn't break ....
2. you (f.) didn't laugh .... 7. you (f.) didn't drink ....
3. you (pl.) didn't fail .... 8. you (pl.) didn't open ....
4. they didn't explain .... 9. they didn't touch ....
5. we didn't write .... 10. we didn't steal ....

6. Complete the following verb tables with negative perfect forms.

	didn't do	didn't play
ána		
íḥna		
ínta		
ínti		
íntu		
húwwa		
híyya		
húmma		

7. Circle the words to complete the following sentences.

The negative of perfect verbs is formed by adding (1. a prefix / a suffix / a prefix and a suffix). When the positive perfect form ends in a vowel, the vowel is (2. lengthened / assimilated / elided) before the suffix -ʃ. This is the case for the following persons: (3. ána / íḥna / ínta / ínti / íntu / húwwa / híyya / húmma). When the positive perfect form ends in two consonants, adding the suffix -ʃ would result in three adjacent consonants. As this is not allowed in ECA, the vowel (4. a / i / u) is inserted before -sh. This is the case for the following

12 Egyptian Colloquial Arabic Verbs Exercise Book

persons: (5. ána / íħna / ínta / ínti / íntu / húwwa / híyya / húmma). The stressed syllabe shifts in all persons except those for which the positive form ends in (6. a vowel / two adjacent consonants / -it).

8. Complete the following table with personal and negative affixes. The first is done for you.

	negative perfect
ána	ma-____-tiʃ
íħna	
ínta	
ínti	
íntu	
húwwa	
híyya	
húmma	

9. Chain Transformation Drill: Change the verb into the form indicated in parantheses. Use your answer as the verb to transform in the next problem. The first three are done for you.

ʃírib

1. (híyya)	ʃírbit	11. (híyya)	....
2. (negative)	maʃirbítʃ	12. (húmma)	....
3. (íħna)	maʃribnāʃ	13. (positive)	....
4. (positive)	....	14. (húwwa)	....
5. (write)	....	15. (ána)	....
6. (húmma)	....	16. (ínta)	....
7. (negative)	....	17. (negative)	....
8. (íntu)	....	18. (do)	....
9. (ínta)	....	19. (híyya)	....
10. (get dressed)	....	20. (understand)	....

Section 5: The Positive Imperfect Tense

Good job! Let's move on to the non-perfect tenses, namely the imperfect, as well as the bi-imperfect and future tenses, which are based on it. The same personal suffixes are used for all sound verbs in non-perfect tenses. It is the sound changes that you will need to watch out for. See p. 12-15.

1. Look at the positive imperfect of verb tables 1s1-6. Change the following perfect verbs into the imperfect. Each problem's number corresponds to its verb's table.

1. ḍárab	....	3. mísik	....
2. kátab	....	4. síkin	....
5. ṭálab	....	6. ʃírib	....

2. Using your answers from exercise 1, and without looking back at the verb tables, change the following perfect verbs into the imperfect. As in exercise 1, the number corresponds to the verb's table.

1. ħáḍar	....	3. dáxal	....
2. lámas	....	4. fíhim	....
5. líbis	....	6. síkit	....

3. Circle the words to complete the following sentences.

The base form *(Remember: that's the **húwwa** form of the positive perfect tense.)* contains two vowels which separate the three radicals of a sound form I verb. These two vowels are both either **a** or **i** (or in some instances **u**). The imperfect tense is created by (1. removing / changing) the first vowel, making the first and second radicals adjacent to each other. The second vowel (2. always / sometimes / never) changes, as is the case for verbs of the following tables: (3. 1s1, 1s2, 1s3, 1s4, 1s5, 1s6). However, the vowel remains the same for verbs of the following tables: 1s1, 1s2, 1s3, 1s4, 1s5, 1s6. This vowel determines the vowel which appears in the personal (5. prefix / suffix) of the imperfect tense. If the vowel is **a** or **i**, the prefix will contain (6. a / i / u), and if the vowel is **u**, the prefix will contain (7. a / i / u).

4. Complete the table by writing in the vowels which are found in tables 1s1-1s6. 'C' stands for consonant and represents the radicals. Mark the stressed syllable.

table	perfect húwwa form	imperfect húwwa form
1s1	C.....C.....C	y.....CC.....C
1s2	C.....C.....C	y.....CC.....C
1s3	C.....C.....C	y.....CC.....C
1s4	C.....C.....C	y.....CC.....C
1s5	C.....C.....C	y.....CC.....C
1s6	C.....C.....C	y.....CC.....C

5. Now that we are aware of the similarities and differences between tables 1s1-6, let's go back and put all the verbs seen in the exercises thus far into groups according to which tables they belong to. Use the Verb Index by Table (p. 120) and/or the Verb Index by Transcription (p.141). And while you're at it, write each verb's translation next to it. The first one is done for you on the following page.

ʔáʒad	gáma3	láħam	ríkib	wáṣaf
bá3at	yásal	lámas	sáraʔ	wáṣal
báħas	ħáḍar	lí3ib	síkin	wázan
dáfa3	ħálaʔ	líbis	síkit	wílid
dáras	ħáras	mísik	sími3	xárag
dáxal	ħásab	náfa3	ṣáraf	3ámal
díħik	ħílim	náṭaʔ	ʃákar	3írif
ḍárab	kánas	nízil	ʃáraħ	3íṭis
fátaħ	kásar	ráʔaṣ	ʃírib	
fíhim	kátab	rákan	ṭábax	
fíʃil	kíbir	rásam	ṭálab	

1s1 .... **1s3** ....

.... **1s2** ....ʔá3ad..=..sit............ ....

....

....

....

....

....

.... **1s5**

....

....

.... **1s4** ....

....

.... **1s6**

....

....

....

6. Oral: Use the table in exercise 4 to change the verbs in exercise 5 into the imperfect tense. Do not write your answers, but rather say them aloud.

A common use of the imperfect tense is to follow a precursor (see p. 103). Let's use the precursors **lāzim** (need) and **3āyiz** (want) in the following exercise.

Examples:	lāzim yíktib.	*He needs to write.*
	3āyiz yíktib.	*He wants to write.*

7. Translate the following.

1. lāzim yídris ....
2. 3āyiz yíʃraḥ ....
3. lāzim yílbis ....

4. 3āyiz yúrʔuş ....
5. lāzim yúskut ....
6. 3āyiz yíʃrab ....

The **híyya** form simply replaces the **y-** in the prefix with **t-**. Notice that, while **lāzim** is invariable for gender or number, **3āyiz** has a feminine form: **3áyza**.

Examples:	lāzim tíktib.	*She needs to write.*
	3áyza tíktib.	*She wants to write.*

---

8. Translate the following.

1. She wants to play. ....
2. She needs to understand. ....
3. She wants to hear. ....

4. She wants to give birth. ....
5. She needs to know. ....
6. She needs to exit. ....

The **ínta** form is identical to the **híyya** form. This may seem confusing, but context, and words such as precursors with feminine forms, will make it clear which person is being referred to.

---

9. Multiple Choice.

1. lāzim túdxul *a. She needs to enter.* *b. You (m.) need to enter.* *c. both a and b*
2. 3áyza túxrug *a. She wants to exit.* *b. You (m.) want to exit.* *c. both a and b*
3. lāzim tírkin *a. She needs to park.* *b. You (m.) need to park.* *c. both a and b*
4. 3āyiz túknus *a. She wants to sweep.* *b. You (m.) want to sweep.* *c. both a and b*
5. 3āyiz tílmis *a. She wants to touch.* *b. You (m.) want to touch.* *c. both a and b*
6. lāzim tíbḥas *a. She needs to research.* *b. You (m.) need to research.* *c. both a and b*

The **íḥna** form begins with **n-**. The precursor **3āyiz** takes the plural form **3ayzīn**.

10. Translate the following.

1. 3ayzīn núrʔuş ....
2. 3āyiz tílbis ....
3. 3áyza tídḥak ....
4. lāzim núskut ....

5. 3āyiz yíʃrab ....
6. lāzim tídris ....
7. 3ayzīn níʃrab ....
8. lāzim yíbḥas ....

---

11. Translate the following.

1. He wants to dream. ....
2. You (m.) need to collect. ....
3. We want to collect. ....
4. She needs to dream. ....

5. She wants to study. ....
6. You (m.) want to study. ....
7. We need to cook. ....
8. He needs to cook. ....

The **ána** form is **a-**, and the **-i-/-u-** present in other imperfect prefixes is assimilated. The invariable precursor **múmkin** means *might*.

12. Translate the following.

1. lāzim ádris ....
2. múmkin áṭbux ....

3. 3āyiz árʔuṣ ....
4. múmkin áʃrab ....

In exercise 12, number 3, the precursor **3āyiz** is masculine. However, **ána** can also be feminine, in which case number 3 would be **3áyza árʔuṣ** since the precursor varies for gender. Two more variable precursors are **nāwi** (intend to) and **musta3ídd** (be willing to).

	masculine	feminine	plural
want to	**3āyiz**	**3áyza**	**3ayzīn**
intend to	**nāwi**	**náwya**	**nawyīn**
be willing to	**musta3ídd**	**musta3ídda**	**musta3iddīn**
need to	**lāzim**	**lāzim**	**lāzim**

13. Translate the following.

1. I (m.) am willing to cook. ....
2. I (f.) am willing to cook. ....
3. you (m.) intend to study. ....
4. you (f.) intend to study. ....

5. I (f.) want to drink. ....
6. I (f.) need to research. ....
7. We intend to drink. ....
8. I (m.) intend to be quiet. ....

14. So far we have learned the imperfect tense conjugations for five persons. Fill out these personal prefixes in the table below, and then complete the table after studying tables 1s1-1s6. The íħna forms have been done for you.

	positive imperfect
ána	
íħna	*ní-___ / nú-___*
ínta	
ínti	
íntu	
húwwa	
híyya	
húmma	

15. Translate the following.

1. lāzim tidrísi ....
2. 3ayzīn níʃraħ ....
3. musta3iddīn tilbísu ....

4. 3áyza túrʔuṣ ....
5. 3áyza turʔúṣi ....
6. nawyīn yiʃrábu ....

16. Translate the following.

1. you (m.) need to study ....
2. we need to explain ....
3. you (pl.) want to get dressed ....

4. she needs to dance ....
5. you (f.) intend to dance ....
6. I intend to drink ....

17. Identify which four of the following nine verbal phrases are grammatically incorrect.

1. 3āyiz tidrísi
2. 3ayzīn núrʔuş
3. nawyīn tilbísu

4. nāwi yiʃrábu
5. lāzima turʔúşi
6. musta3iddīn yiʃrábu

7. 3āyiz túrʔuş
8. 3áyza túrʔuş
9. lāzim niʃrábi

18. Complete the following verb tables with positive imperfect forms.

	fíhim	fátaḥ	dáxal
ána			
íḥna			
ínta			
ínti			
íntu			
húwwa			
híyya			
húmma			

Section 6: The Negative Imperfect Tense

The negative imperfect tense is not commonly used, and will therefore be dealt with briefly here. It is most commonly used as the negative imperative, which will be explored in part 7. The negative imperfect is formed by adding the prefix ma- and the suffix -ʃ to the positive form. This causes various sound changes.

1. Use table 1s1 to complete the table below with the positive and negative forms of the verb kásar (break). Be sure to mark the stressed syllable.

	positive	negative
ána		
íḥna		
ínta		
ínti		
íntu		
húwwa		
híyya		
húmma		

2. All but one of verbs in the following table are incorrect. Find and correct the mistakes. (wáṣaf = describe)

	incorrect	corrected
ána	māwṣáfʃ	
íḥna	maníwṣafʃ	
ínta	matiwṣáfʃ	
ínti	matiwṣafíʃ	
íntu	matiwṣáfūʃ	
húwwa	mawaṣáfʃ	
híyya	mayiwṣáfʃ	
húmma	mayiṣafūʃ	

3. Put the following verbs into the negative form.

1. yíb3at   ....
2. nídris   ....
3. túxrug   ....
4. áfʃal   ....
5. tilbísi   ....
6. yuskútu   ....
7. yiʃrábu   ....
8. tisráʔu   ....
9. tuknúsu   ....
10. áḥsib   ....

11. tílmis   ....
12. tismá3u ....
13. níkbar   ....
14. tirkíni ....
15. áʃrab   ....
16. tuʃkúru ....
17. yigmá3u ....
18. tiṣrífi ....
19. níḥḍar   ....
20. tídḥak   ....

---

lāzim, as you learned in part 6, can translate as *need to*. It can also translate as *have to* and *must*. These two synonyms have different meanings when made negative (*don't have to* and *mustn't*) in English. Similarly, **lāzim** + imperfect can be made negative in two ways to express these meanings.

lāzim yí3mil	*he needs to do, he has to do, he must do*
miʃ lāzim yí3mil	*he doesn't need to do, he doesn't have to do*
lāzim mayi3mílʃ	*he mustn't do*

---

4. Translate the following.

1. lāzim ádris
2. lāzim maniḍrábʃ
3. miʃ lāzim tiʃrábi

4. miʃ lāzim tífham
5. lāzim mayuṭbuxūʃ
6. lāzim mayiktíbʃ

5. Translate the following.

1. you (f.) don't have to study
2. you (m.) mustn't hit
3. you (pl.) mustn't drink

4. we don't need to play
5. she has to understand
6. he mustn't sit

Section 7: The Imperative

1. Fill in the tables below with the positive imperfect and positive imperative forms using tables 1s1-3. Then answer the following question.

	1s1 ḍárab		1s2 kátab		1s3 ṭálab	
	imperfect	*imperative*	*imperfect*	*imperative*	*imperfect*	*imperative*
ínta						
ínti						
íntu						

1. What is the only difference between the positive imperfect forms and the positive imperative forms?

2. Translate the following as if you were speaking to one man, one woman, and a group of people.

1. Do!   ....
2. Study!   ....
3. Explain!   ....
4. Be quiet! ....
5. Sit!   ....
6. Listen!   ....

3. Compare the negative imperfect forms to the negative imperative forms in tables 1s1-1s6. Then answer the following question.

1. How are the negative imperfect forms different from the negative imperative forms?

4. Translate the following as if you were speaking to one man, one woman, and a group of people.

1. Don't steal!   ....
2. Don't pay!   ....
3. Don't enter!   ....
4. Don't laugh!   ....
5. Don't sit!   ....

5. Chain Transformation Drill.

íʃrab

1. (ínti)	....	11. (*study*)	....
2. (negative)	....	12. (ínti)	....
3. (ínta)	....	13. (íntu)	....
4. (*do*)	....	14. (positive)	....
5. (positive)	....	15. (*ride*)	....
6. (íntu)	....	16. (negative)	....
7. (ínti)	....	17. (ínti)	....
8. (*exit*)	....	18. (ínta)	....
9. (negative)	....	19. (positive)	....
10. (ínta)	....	20. (*drink*)	....

Section 8: The Future Tense

1. Look at the verb tables to answer the following questions.

1. What is the future tense prefix?
2. The future tense is formed by adding the prefix to which verb tense?
3. What happens to the vowel of the prefix in the first person singular (ána) form?
4. How is the negative future formed?

2. Translate the following.

1. ḥárʔuṣ	....	5. ḥatilbísu	....
2. miʃ ḥaníʃraḥ	....	6. miʃ ḥayí3mil	....
3. ḥatírkab	....	7. ḥatírkin	....
4. ḥatidrísi	....	8. miʃ ḥayiʃrábu	....

3. Translate the following.

1. you (m.) won't exit	....	4. she won't listen	....
2. we will pay	....	5. I will play	....
3. you (pl.) will be quiet	....	6. they won't fail	....

Section 9: The Positive Bi-Imperfect Tense

1. Look at verb tables 1s1-1s6 to answer the following questions.

1. How does the bi-imperfect differ from the (bare) imperfect?
2. Is the i of the bi- prefix ever assimilated?
3. Does the i of the bi- prefix become bu- before verbs which have u in the personal prefix?

2. Change the following bare imperfect verbs into bi-imperfect verbs.

1. yíḍrab	....	4. ámsik	....
2. tífham	....	5. yiktíbu	....
3. núdxul	....	6. yíʃrab	....

3. Complete the following verb tables with bi-imperfect verbs without looking back at the verb tables in the book. If you're having trouble, look back at previous exercises to help you.

	ʃírib	kátab	ṭálab
ána			
íḥna			
ínta			
ínti			
íntu			
húwwa			
híyya			
húmma			

The bi-imperfect can refer to habitual actions or general truths, translating as the present simple tense in English. It can also refer to actions happening at the present moment, as does the present continuous tense in English.

Example: biyíʃrab.   He drinks. (present simple)
                         He is drinking. (present continuous)

---

4. Translate your answers from exercise 2 into the present simple tense of English.

1. ……………………………………   4. …………………………………….
2. ……………………………………   5. …………………………………….
3. ……………………………………

5. Translate the following into the present continuous tense of English.

1. biní3mil   ……………………………………   4. biyírkab   ………………………………………….
2. bádris   ……………………………………   5. biyiktíbu   ………………………………………….
3. bitirkíni   ……………………………………

If the preceding word—usually the subject of the verb—ends in a vowel, elision of the i of the bi- prefix becomes possible. (See **Vowel Elision** p. 13) This is the case with pronoun subjects, which are used for emphasis. Notice the elision in the example below.

Compare: biyíktib.   He writes.
                       húwwa byíktib.   *He* writes. (It is *he* who writes, and not someone else.)

---

6. Complete the following table with the bi-imperfect forms of the verb dáras (study) preceded by a subject pronoun for emphasis.

dáras (study)
ána
íḥna
ínta
ínti
íntu
húwwa
híyya
húmma

7. Following the pattern in the example, make sentences with the names and verbs provided. If you are unsure of the gender of a name, refer to appendix A in the back of the exercise book (p. 94). Pay attention to whether the name ends in a vowel or consonant to determine whether elision occurs or not.

Example: (dáras) áḥmad, 3áli
áḥmad biyídris wi 3áli byídris kamān. (Ahmed is studying, and Ali is studying, too.)

1. (3ámal) karīm, nágwa ....wi...kamān.....
2. (lí3ib) sāmi, sāmiḥ ....
3. (báḥas) zēnab, 3azīza ....
4. (ɣásal) 3abīr, hāni ....
5. (líbis) múṣṭafa, fáṭma ....

Section 10: The Negative Bi-Imperfect Tense

If you look at the verb tables, you'll see that the bi-imperfect is negated in the same way as the bare imperfect and perfect tenses—with a combination of the prefix ma- and the suffix -ʃ. The suffix -ʃ causes the same sound changes that occur in the negative bare imperfect, while the prefix **ma-** affects the **i** of the prefix **bi-** in the same way that a preceding word ending in a vowel does—the **i** of **bi-** is elided.

1. Make the following verbs negative and then translate as the present simple in English.

1. biyúṭbux ....
2. bitíʃrab ....
3. biyi3ráfu ....
4. biní3mil ....
5. bitidfá3i ....

6. bitidḥáku ....
7. bársim ....
8. biyíftaḥ ....
9. bitísraʔ ....
10. bitúḥrus ....

2. Put the following verbs into the first-person singular (ána) form of the negative bi-imperfect tense.

1. síkit ....
2. líbis ....
3. sími3 ....

4. ɣásal ....
5. ʃákar ....
6. ḥálaʔ ....

3. Put the following verbs into the first-person plural (íḥna) form of the negative bi-imperfect tense.

1. wáṣaf ....
2. ɣásal ....
3. sími3 ....
4. síkin ....
5. ʃákar ....
6. ḥála? ....

4. Put the following verbs into the second-person masculine singular (ínta) form of the negative bi-imperfect tense.

1. síkin ....
2. gáma3 ....
3. wáṣaf ....
4. ɣásal ....
5. náṭa? ....
6. ḥála? ....

5. Put the following verbs into the second-person feminine singular (ínti) form of the negative bi-imperfect tense.

1. gáma3 ....
2. wáṣaf ....
3. síkin ....
4. ḥílim ....
5. kánas ....
6. náṭa? ....

6. Put the following verbs into the second-person plural (íntu) form of the negative bi-imperfect tense.

1. ḥílim ....
2. kánas ....
3. kátab ....
4. gáma3 ....
5. láḥam ....
6. náṭa? ....

7. Put the following verbs into the third-person masculine singular (húwwa) form of the negative bi-imperfect tense.

1. ḥílim ....
2. kánas ....
3. fíʃil ....
4. fátaḥ ....
5. kátab ....
6. láḥam ....

8. Put the following verbs into the third-person feminine singular (híyya) form of the negative bi-imperfect tense.

1. wílid ....
2. fíʃil ....
3. láḥam ....
4. fátaḥ ....
5. kátab ....
6. ríkib ....

9. Put the following verbs into the third-person plural (húmma) form of the negative bi-imperfect tense.

1. fátaḥ ....
2. dáras ....
3. wílid ....
4. ríkib ....
5. kásar ....
6. fíʃil ....

10. Translate the following.

1. I don't drink ....
2. Yūsif doesn't know ....
3. Márwa doesn't do ....
4. You (pl.) don't know ....
5. We don't open ....

6. Yásmin and Farīda aren't laughing ....
7. I don't steal ....
8. You (f.) don't pay ....
9. He doesn't know ....
10. You (m.) don't guard ....

Section 11: The Active Participle

1. Circle the words to complete the following sentences.

The active participle follows (1. identical / different) patterns for 1s1-1s6 verbs. The masculine form inserts (2. ā / ī / ū) between the first and second radicals, while there is (3. a / i / nothing) between the second and third radicals. The feminine form adds the suffix (4. -a / -i / -it). This makes it possible to (5. shorten / elide / lengthen) the vowel in the preceding syllable, which in turn requires the vowel of the first syllable to (6. shorten / elide / lengthen). The plural form adds the suffix (7. -ān / -īn / -ūn) to the masculine form, which has (8. the same / a different) effect on the preceding vowels, except that the stress moves to the (9. final / second to final) syllable.

> The active participle has several uses. The first is that it can be used as an adjective, and commonly translates as the gerund, that is, verb + -ing, in English.

2. Translate the following as the gerund in English.

1. 3āmil ....
2. dāris ....
3. kātib ....

4. 3ārif ....
5. sākin ....
6. lābis ....

3. Translate the following as masculine singular active participles.

1. opening ....
2. washing ....
3. riding ....

4. sitting ....
5. understanding ....
6. exiting ....

4. Change your answers from exercise 3 into the feminine singular form.

1. ....
2. ....
3. ....

4. ....
5. ....
6. ....

5. Change the following verbs into plural active participles.

1. ḥáḍar ....
2. nízil ....
3. ṭálab ....

4. dáxal ....
5. lí3ib ....
6. ʔá3ad ....

Another use of the active participle is to express a completed action. This corresponds to the present perfect tense of English.

Examples:
áḥmad kātib gawāb.   Aḥmad has written a letter.
sāra líssa kátba gawāb.   Sāra has just written a letter.

Because active participles only show gender and number, but not person, a subject pronoun is *required* in the absence of a noun subject.

Examples:
húwwa kātib gawāb.   He has written a letter.
ínta kātib gawāb.   You (m.) have written a letter.

The first-person singular (**ána**) is non-gender specific in other tenses. However, a speaker must specify his or her gender with a masculine or feminine active participle.

Examples:
ána kātib gawāb.   I (m.) have written a letter.
ána kátba gawāb.   I (f.) have written a letter.

The active participle is made negative with **miʃ**.

Example: húwwa miʃ kātib gawāb.   He hasn't written a letter.

6. Translate the following.

1. We've failed. ……………………………………
2. You (m.) have swept. ……………………………
3. He's just shaven. ………………………………
4. Fáṭma hasn't paid. ……………………………
5. I (f.) have opened. ……………………………

6. They have just explained. ………………………
7. I (m.) have just done. ……………………………
8. You (f.) haven't swept. …………………………
9. You (pl.) have just opened. ……………………
10. Karīm hasn't shaven. …………………………

A third use of the active participle will be introduced later.

Section 12: The Passive Participle

The passive participle acts as an adjective. As such, it has three forms: masculine, feminine, and plural. It corresponds to the past participle in English.

Examples:
3árabi -lmaktūb   written Arabic
fawātīr madfū3a   paid bills

1. Study the passive participle in verb tables 1s1-6. Then complete the following table with forms of the passive participle.

	ʃírib	*kásar*	*wílid*
masc.			
fem.			
plural			

2. Wordsearch: Find the past participles of the following verbs in the wordsearch puzzle and write them in the correct column below.

dáfa3	ɣásal	kátab	wázan
dáras	ḥáras	rásam	wílid
fíhim	kásar	síkin	3írif

n	m	m	r	ʃ	w	m	a	ū	m	m	x	l	m	s	x	ẓ
m	m	a	d	r	ū	s	a	m	a	a	ḍ	m	a	r	l	i
z	i	w	k	i	ṭ	a	m	k	a	f	ħ	ū	k	n	z	m
m	a	l	ū	t	a	m	t	ā	s	h	a	r	s	ū	n	a
a	a	u	ū	ḍ	u	ū	a	ṭ	ā	ū	k	i	u	k	ā	w
ħ	ʃ	d	g	ā	b	s	a	r	n	m	r	b	n	s	y	z
r	r	ī	f	b	a	r	m	ū	s	a	a	a	i	a	ī	u
u	ṣ	n	ħ	ū	m	a	k	s	r	ī	n	f	n	m	b	n
s	i	k	i	n	3	m	i	m	a	ɣ	s	u	l	ī	n	ī
i	ṭ	m	a	r	r	ū	g	m	a	d	r	u	s	n	a	n
m	a	w	ū	z	i	n	w	a	ṣ	ā	ɣ	m	a	m	r	l
m	a	f	h	u	m	a	ɣ	s	ū	l	a	ʃ	ẓ	x	m	f
k	a	t	a	b	f	u	r	3	a	m	a	f	h	m	ī	n

masculine	feminine	plural
…………………………	…………………………	…………………………
…………………………	…………………………	…………………………
…………………………	…………………………	…………………………
…………………………	…………………………	…………………………

Section 13: Review of Part 1

1. The following verb table contains various sound measure I verbs, but with many mistakes. Cross out the incorrect forms and write their correct forms to their right.

	positive	negative	
ána	darást	marakántʃ	**perfect**
íħna	sikína	mamsiknāʃ	
ínta	lámast	makasártiʃ	
ínti	3irífti	mafhimtíʃ	
íntu	katábtū	masaraʔtūʃ	
húwwa	ʃárab	maħilímʃ	
híyya	nízilit	masím3ítʃ	
húmma	dáfa3u	mayiħsibūʃ	

ána	ágma3	maanfá3ʃ	**imperfect**
íħna	náħras	manibħásʃ	
ínta	tídħak	matiḍrábʃ	
ínti	tidħákti	matiwṣalīʃ	
íntu	tidxílu	matirkibūʃ	
húwwa	yúkbur	mayba3átʃ	
híyya	tílbis	matúrʔuṣʃ	
húmma	yiṣrífu	mayilħímu	

ána	báħḍar	mabawṣífʃ	**bi-imperfect**
íħna	baníl3ab	mabniyṣálʃ	
ínta	bitíḍrab	matuʔ3údiʃ	
ínti	bitúskut	mabṭutbuxīʃ	
íntu	bitiftáħu	mabtuxrugūʃ	
húwwa	biywízin	mabyí3milʃ	
híyya	bitúknus	mabtuṭlúbʃ	
húmma	biyiʃráħu	mabyiʃʃalūʃ	

ána	xársim	maħarsímʃ	**future**
íħna	níħlaʔ	miʃ níħlaʔ	
ínta	ħatí3ṭis	miʃ ħatí3ṭas	
ínti	ħitinṭáʔi	miʃ ħatinṭáʔi	
íntu	ħatuskúnu	miʃ ħatuskúnu	
húwwa	ħayíkbar	miʃ yíkbar	
híyya	ħatíwlid	miʃ ħayíwlid	
húmma	ħayiʃrábu	miʃ ħayiʃrábu	

ínta	tíktib	matiktíbʃ	**imperative**
ínti	údxuli	madxulīʃ	
íntu	idfá3u	matidfa3ūʃ	

	active	passive	
masculine	kātib	miʃ kātib	**participles**
feminine	katība	maḍrūba	
plural	katbīn	mawlūdin	

2. Read the following and mark x's on the chart.

áḥmad mabyiktíbʃ. máryam mabtiʃrábʃ. 3áli wi múna mabyiktibūʃ. áḥmad wi máryam mabyuṭbuxūʃ. 3áli mabyiʃrábʃ. múna mabtuṭbúxʃ.

	writing	cooking	drinking
3áli			
máryam			
áḥmad			
múna			

Look at the chart and write a sentence for each verb in the positive bi-imperfect tense.

1. ....
2. ....
3. ....

3. Translate the following.

1. She sent.   ....
2. He'll study.   ....
3. living (f.)   ....
4. They want to play.   ....
5. He steals.   ....
6. We won't research.   ....
7. I didn't touch.   ....
8. She doesn't do.   ....
9. written (m.)   ....
10. You (pl.) need to know...............................

11. I want to thank.   ....
12. They just cooked.   ....
13. You (m.) don't open.   ....
14. We exited.   ....
15. Don't write! (f.)   ....
16. It (m.) is useful.   ....
17. Dance! (pl.)   ....
18. 3áli is sneezing.   ....
19. You (f.) didn't attend. ....
20. They rode.   ....

Part 2: Non-Sound Measure I Verbs

Section 1: The Hollow Verb

1. Look up the following verbs in the indexes and rewrite them in the correct column below. Write each verb's translation next to it.

ʔāl	fāt	nām	ṭār	3āʃ
bās	gāb	rāḥ	xāf	
bāt	kān	sāb	zār	
bā3	māt	ʃāf	3ām	

1h1 ....

....

.... **1h3**

.... **1h2** ....

....

.... **1h4**

....

2. Translate the following forms of the perfect tense.

1. rāḥ ....
2. bāsit ....
3. gābu ....
4. ṭārit ....
5. 3āmu ....

6. maráḥʃ ....
7. mabasítʃ ....
8. magabūʃ ....
9. maṭárʃ ....
10. ma3ámʃ ....

3. Translate the following.

1. he saw ....
2. they visited ....
3. she said ....
4. she slept ....
5. they sold ....

6. he didn't see ....
7. they didn't visit ....
8. she didn't say ....
9. she didn't sleep ....
10. they didn't sell ....

4. Translate the following forms of the perfect tense. Notice that the ā changes to a short vowel, either i or u in the first and second person forms.

1. ʃúfna ....
2. zúrtu ....
3. ʔult ....
4. nímti ....

5. bi3t ....
6. maxufnāʃ ....
7. marúḥtiʃ ....
8. magibtūʃ ....

5. Look at the verbs in exercise 4. For which tables does the ā change to i and for which does it change to u in the first and second person forms? Check the boxes in the table below. Then fill in the missing vowels from the verbs.

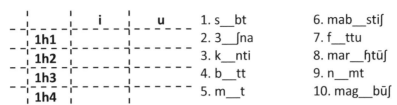

	i	u
1h1		
1h2		
1h3		
1h4		

1. s__bt
2. 3__ʃna
3. k__nti
4. b__tt
5. m__t

6. mab__stiʃ
7. f__ttu
8. mar__ḥtūʃ
9. n__mt
10. mag__būʃ

6. Now that we've become familiar with the forms of hollow verbs in the perfect tense, let's turn our attention to forms in the imperfect, bi-imperfect, and future tenses. Match the verb forms on the left to their translations.

1. 3āyiz anām	I want to sleep
2. binzūr	I'll go
3. bagīb	he isn't afraid
4. ḥarūḥ	I bring / I'm bringing
5. lazim matbi3īʃ	she doesn't want to say
6. miʃ 3áyza tʔūl	you (f.) musn't sell
7. biysību	we visit / we're visiting
8. mabiyxáfʃ	they leave / they're leaving
9. miʃ 3āyiz tiʔūl	you (m.) don't want to say

7. Look back at the forms in exercise 6. The imperfect, bi-imperfect, and future tenses each contain a long vowel which is shortened when the negative -ʃ suffix is added. Which tables contain each vowel?

1. ā/a   ....
2. ī/i   ....
3. ū/u   ....

> In sound verbs, the personal prefix is followed by two adjacent consonants (radicals). This protects the vowel of the personal prefix from being elided, as elision would result in three adjacent consonants, which is not allowed. However, in hollow verbs, the second radical is a vowel (which can be shortened but is usually not elided). This allows the **i** of the personal prefix to elide when preceded by a vowel, as in the examples below. (See p. 12 for more information on elision.)
>
> bi + yigīb → biygīb
>
> húwwa + yigīb → húwwa ygīb
>
> ma + yigīb + ʃ → maygíbʃ
>
> ḥa + yigīb → ḥaygīb

8. Cross out the vowels which can be elided.

1. manigíbʃ
2. mabinizúrʃ
3. biyiʔūl
4. mabiyiʔulūʃ
5. mabitinamūʃ
6. bitirūɦ
7. nūra bitirūɦ
8. mabitirúɦʃ
9. nūra mabitirúɦʃ

9. Multiple choice. Choose the correct form.

1. he goes
   a. biyirūɦ   b. byirūɦ   c. biyrūɦ   d. byrūɦ

2. she doesn't swim
   a. mabti3úmʃ   b. mabit3úmʃ   c. mabt3úmʃ   d. mabiti3úmʃ

3. we will bring
   a. ɦanigīb   b. ɦangīb   c. ɦanigb   d. ɦanīgb

4. 3áli says
   a. 3áli biyʔūl   b. 3áli biyiʔūl   c. 3áli byʔūl   d. 3áli byiʔūl

5. they don't go
   a. mabiyiruɦūʃ   b. mabiyruɦūʃ   c. mabyiruɦūʃ   d. mabyirɦūʃ

10. Look at verb tables 1h1-4 and fill in the table below with the table the imperative forms of rāɦ. Then answer the questions.

	positive	negative
ínta		
ínti		
íntu		

1. How would you translate the positive forms? ………………….……………..
2. How about the negative forms? …………………….……………..

11. Translate the following as if you were speaking to one man, one woman, and a group of people.

1. Swim!   ………………………………   ………………………………   ………………………………
2. Don't sleep!   ………………………………   ………………………………   ………………………………
3. Bring!   ………………………………   ………………………………   ………………………………
4. Don't be!   ………………………………   ………………………………   ………………………………
5. Be afraid!   ………………………………   ………………………………   ………………………………
6. Don't sell!   ………………………………   ………………………………   ………………………………

12. Look at verb tables 1h1-4 and fill in the table below with the table the active and passive participles of bā3.

	active	passive
masculine		
feminine		
plural		

13. Translate the following.

1. he was	....	6. he didn't die	....
2. they kissed	....	7. you (m.) don't visit	....
3. they'll swim	....	8. we need to sell	....
4. you (m.) don't sleep	....	9. they stay overnight	....
5. she wants to fly	....	10. Múna lives	....

You learned that the bi-imperfect translates in English as both the present simple tense and present continuous tense. However, for verbs of motion and location, the bi-imperfect is only used to express habitual actions (present simple), while the active participle, preceded by a subject (noun or pronoun), expresses an action at the time of speaking.

Compare: **bitrūħ** ilmadrása kúllə yōm.   **She goes** to school every day.

híyya **ráyħa** ilmadrása dilwáʔti.   **She's going** to school now.

14. Translate the following with the present simple and present continuous tenses in English.

1. sāmi rāyiħ	....	7. ána miʃ rāyiħ	....
2. biyrūħ	....	8. mabarúħʃ	....
3. híyya ráyħa	....	9. rīm miʃ ráyħa	....
4. rīm bitrūħ	....	10. húmma rayħīn	....
5. íntu rayħīn	....	11. ínti ráyħa	....
6. biyrūħu	....	12. mabiyruħūʃ	....

Section 2: The Defective Verb

1. Look up the following verbs in the indexes and rewrite them in the correct column below. Write each verb's translation next to it.

ʔára	báʔa	hídi	rága
báda	díri	mála	ráma
báka	gára	míʃi	ṣíħi
bána	gíri	nísi	3áfa

1d1   **1d2**   ....

....   **1d3**   ....

....

....   **1d4**   **1d5**

....

....

2. Look at tables 1d1-3 to translate the following.

1. she filled ....
2. they threw ....
3. she implored ....
4. they filled ....
5. she began ....

6. they built ....
7. he cried ....
8. they forgave ....
9. she became ....
10. it (f.) happened ....

3. Look at tables 1d4-5 to translate the following.

1. she realized ....
2. they forgot ....
3. she woke up ....

4. they walked ....
5. he ran ....
6. they ran ....

4. Translate the following.

1. hídyit ....
2. ʔaru ....
3. maʔarūʃ ....
7. mahdīʃ ....
8. manisyítʃ ....

4. mamalāʃ ....
5. báʔit ....
6. mabaʔūʃ ....
9. manisyūʃ ....
10. maramūʃ ....

5. Look at tables 1d1-5 to translate the following. Notice that the final -a or i of defective verbs is replaced by a long vowel in the first and second person forms.

1. I filled ....
2. you (m.) threw ....
3. we forgot ....
4. you (f.) ran ....
5. I woke up ....

6. you (pl.) walked ....
7. you (pl.) forgave ....
8. you (m.) cried ....
9. we were quiet ....
10. you (f.) built ....

6. Below are examples of negative defective verbs. Notice that the -ʃ suffix causes the long vowel to shorten, which usually results in a short vowel becoming a candidate for elision. Remember that a short i or u may be a candidate, while a short a can never be elided. Often there is more than one candidate for elision, in which case it is the first candidate which is elided. Cross out the vowels which can be elided in the verbs below, and then translate.

1. maramítʃ ....
2. mamalināʃ ....
3. maragitīʃ ....

4. manisīʃ ....
5. maʔaritūʃ ....
6. mamiʃyítʃ ....

7. magiryūʃ ....
8. mabadināʃ ....
9. maṣiħīʃ ....

7. Change your answers from exercise 5 into the negative.

1. ....
2. ....
3. ....
4. ....
5. ....

6. ....
7. ....
8. ....
9. ....
10. ....

8. Oral: Translate the following. Do not write your answers, but rather say them aloud.

1. I read
2. I didn't read
3. you (m.) read
4. we didn't read
5. she ran
6. they didn't run
7. he realized
8. you (pl.) didn't realize
9. you (f.) cried
10. you (m.) didn't cry

9. Chain Transformation Drill. The first one is done for you.

báʔa

1. (negative)   *mabaʔāʃ*
2. (híyya)   ....
3. (ána)   ....
4. (positive)   ....
5. (*wake up*)   ....
6. (húmma)   ....
7. (negative)   ....
8. (*begin*)   ....
9. (ínta)   ....
10. (ínti)   ....
11. (positive)   ....
12. (íɦna)   ....
13. (negative)   ....
14. (*throw*)   ....
15. (húwwa)   ....
16. (*walk*)   ....
17. (positive)   ....
18. (íntu)   ....
19. (híyya)   ....
20. (negative)   ....

10. Now that we've become familiar with the forms of defective verbs in the perfect tense, let's turn our attention to forms in the imperfect, bi-imperfect, and future tenses. Match the verb forms on the left to their translations.

1. 3āyiz amʃi   he doesn't forgive
2. binínsa   I want to walk
3. bárgu   I implore / I'm imploring
4. ɦármi   you (f.) musn't fill
5. lāzim matimlīʃ   I'll throw
6. miʃ 3áyza tíhda   they build / they're building
7. biyíbnu   we forget
8. mabyi3fíʃ   you (m.) don't want to read
9. miʃ 3āyiz tiʔra   she doesn't want to be quiet

11. Look at the verb tables 1d1-5 and the verb indexes on p. 127-128 while circling the words to complete the following sentences and table.

As you know, verb conjugation is based on the húwwa form in Arabic. Let's compare various tenses of measure I defective verbs in the húwwa form to see which vowels are present. If you look at the verb indexes, you will see that the majority of measure I defective verbs belong to table (1. 1d1 / 1d2 / 1d3 / 1d4 / 1d5). For this table, the two vowels in the perfect tense are (2. a and a / a and i / i and i). Now, look at that verb table. In the imperfect tenses, the first vowel disappears so that the two radicals (consonants) are adjacent, and the final vowel is (3. a / i / u). Now look at the preceding verb table. The vowels of both tables are identical in the perfect tense, but in the imperfect tenses, the final vowel is (4. a / i / u). The verb (5. mála / ráma / rága) is irregular, the only verb conjugated according to its table. Its final vowel in the imperfect tenses is (6. a / i / u), and also notice that personal prefix takes the vowel (7. a / i / u), unlike verbs in other tables. Less commonly, perfect verbs may take the vowels (8. a and a / a and i / i and i). The final vowel in the imperfect tenses (9. stays the same as / changes from that of) the final vowel in the perfect tense in the majority of verbs.

12. Translate the following.

1. bábdi ....
2. 3āyiz tígri ....
3. 3áyza tígri ....
4. ḥayíbki ....
5. mabtimʃíʃ ....
6. miʃ ḥayí3fi ....

13. Translate the following.

1. mabaʔrāʃ ....
2. lāzim yínsa ....
3. bitíhda ....
4. mabyidrāʃ ....
5. lāzim mabnimlāʃ ....
6. miʃ ḥayígra ....

14. Look at the imperative forms in tables 1d1-1d5 and translate the following as if you were speaking to one man, one woman, and a group of people.

1. Wake up! ....
2. Don't read! ....
3. Run! ....
4. Don't cry! ....

15. Study the passive participle in verb tables 1d1-5. Then complete the following table with forms of the active and passive participles.

	ʔára	bána	díri	
masc.				active
fem.				active
plural				active
masc.				passive
fem.				passive
plural				passive

16. Oral Chain Transformation Drill. Do not write your answers, but rather say them aloud.

míʃi
1. (negative)
2. (híyya)
3. (húmma)
4. (build)
5. (bi-imperfect)
6. (ínta)
7. (positive)
8. (forget)
9. (negative)
10. (imperative)
11. (positive)
12. (future)
13. (íḥna)
14. (read)
15. (active participle)
16. (híyya)
17. (lāzim)
18. (passive participle)
19. (negative)
20. (ána perfect)

Section 3: The Geminate Verb

1. Use the Verb Index by Table for tables 1g1-3 (p. 128-130) to translate the following.

1. ṣaḥḥ   ....   6. ẓánnu   ....
2. baṣṣ   ....   7. ḥabbēt   ....
3. ḥáttit   ....   8. ḥassēti   ....
4. ráddu   ....   9. mallēna   ....
5. xáʃʃit   ....   10. 3addētu   ....

2. Oral translation.

1. they were appropriate	3. you (m.) put	5. you (f.) entered	7. you (pl.) loved	9. I became bored
	4. we answered	6. she thought	8. he felt	10. she counted
2. I looked				

3. Study the negative forms of the perfect verb in tables 1g1-3. Then translate the following.

1. it wasn't appropriate ....   6. he didn't enter   ....
2. I didn't look   ....   7. you (f.) didn't answer ....
3. she didn't love   ....   8. they didn't count   ....
4. you (m.) didn't become bored.....................   9. I didn't feel   ....
5. we didn't think   ....   10. he didn't put   ....

4. Translate the following.

1. lāzim yiṣáḥḥ   ....   6. 3ayzīn yiẓúnnu   ....
2. náwya tirúdd   ....   7. miʃ 3áyza -búṣṣ   ....
3. 3āyiz yi3ídd   ....   8. miʃ 3ayzīn nimíll   ....
4. musta3iddīn nixúʃʃ ....   9. miʃ lāzim tiḥúṭṭ   ....
5. lāzim aḥíbb   ....   10. nawyīn tiḥíssu   ....

> The conjunction **3aʃān** has two meanings, depending on whether it is followed by the imperfect or the bi-imperfect. Compare the following examples:
>
> | | 3aʃān yiẓúnn | ...so that he thinks |
> |---|---|---|
> | Examples: | 3aʃān mayẓúnniʃ | ... so that he doesn't think |
> | | 3aʃān biyẓúnn | ...because he thinks |
> | | 3aʃān mabyiẓúnniʃ | ...because he doesn't think |

5. Translate the following.

1. 3aʃān tiḥíbbi   ....   6. 3aʃān yiẓúnnu   ....
2. 3aʃānaḥúṭṭ   ....   7. 3aʃān manmílliʃ   ....
3. 3aʃān yi3íddu   ....   8. 3aʃānbitrúdd   ....
4. 3aʃān mabúṣṣiʃ   ....   9. 3aʃān biyṣáḥḥ   ....
5. 3aʃānmababúṣṣiʃ ....   10. 3aʃān mabitxúʃʃūʃ ....

6. Choose the correct form.

1. he feels

     a. biyiħíss   b. byiħíss   c. biyħíss   d. byħíss

2. they don't look

     a. mabyibúṣṣiʃ   b. mabyibuṣṣūʃ   c. mabiybúṣṣuʃ   d. mabiybuṣṣūʃ

3. she will answer

     a. ħatrúdd   b. ħatrúddi   c. ħatirúdd   d. bitrúdd

4. Maħmūd becomes bored

     a. maħmūd biyimíll   b. maħmūd byimíll   c. maħmūd biymíll   d. maħmūd bymíll

5. so that Nūra looks

     a. 3aʃān nūra tibúṣṣ   b. 3aʃān nūra tbúṣṣ   c. 3aʃān nūra btibúṣṣ   d. 3aʃān nūra bitbúṣṣ

6. you (m.) don't love

     a. mabitiħíbbiʃ   b. mabtħíbbiʃ   c. mabitħíbbiʃ   d. mabtiħíbbiʃ

7. Translate the following using the bi-imperfect tense.

1. I love   ....   6. you (pl.) put   ....
2. you (m.) count ....   7. he feels   ....
3. we enter   ....   8. you (m.) become bored ....
4. you (f.) answer ....   9. we wake up   ....
5. they think   ....   10. she looks   ....

8. Oral: Change your answers from exercise 7 into the negative.

9. Translate the following.

1. I won't think   ....   6. you (f.) will enter   ....
2. she will count   ....   7. he won't love   ....
3. we will look   ....   8. you (pl.) will become bored.........................
4. you (m.) will feel   ....   9. I will enter   ....
5. they won't wake up ....   10. he won't look   ....

10. Look at the verb index on p. 127-128 and the imperative forms in tables 1d1-1d5 to translate the following as if you were speaking to one man, one woman, and a group of people.

1. Cut!   ....
2. Don't bite!   ....

3. Solve! ....
4. Don't cheat! ....

11. Study the passive participle in verb tables 1d1-5. Then complete the following table with forms of the active and passive participles.

	ʃakk	sabb	
masc.			active
fem.			active
plural			active
masc.			passive
fem.			passive
plural			passive

12. Change the following verbs in the perfect tense to the bi-imperfect, and the bi-imperfect tense to the perfect.

1. maṣaħħítʃ .... 5. bitrúdd ....
2. ħabbēti .... 6. mabiyħássiʃ ....
3. binħútt .... 7. ma3addūʃ ....
4. ʃakkēt .... 8. ṣammētu ....

Section 4: Review of Section 2

1. Translate the following.

1. I said .... 6. calm down (m.) ....
2. I think .... 7. she doesn't throw ....
3. beginning (f.) .... 8. you (pl.) visit ....
4. they entered .... 9. passing by (m.) ....
5. he didn't feel .... 10. we mustn't see ....

2. Crossword Puzzle: Translate the following.

across:
1. he didn't become bored
2. they didn't wake up
3. you (f.) don't leave
4. I don't read
5. you (f.) mustn't go: lāzim ___
6. she doesn't realize

down:
3. they aren't afraid
7. you (pl.) didn't kiss
8. we didn't build
9. they didn't die

Part 3: A Review of Measure I Verbs

1. Chain Transformation Drill.

kátab

1. (híyya)	....	26. (íntu)	....
2. (*ride*)	....	27. (húmma)	....
3. (húmma)	....	28. (positive)	....
4. (*sell*)	....	29. (bi-imperfect)	....
5. (ána)	....	30. (*count*)	....
6. (negative)	....	31. (húwwa)	....
7. (ínta)	....	32. (imperative m.)	....
8. (ínti)	....	33. (*explain*)	....
9. (*say*)	....	34. (negative)	....
10. (bi-imperfect)	....	35. (perfect)	....
11. (positive)	....	36. (*study*)	....
12. (íḥna)	....	37. (active participle)	....
13. (*fear*)	....	38. (plural)	....
14. (negative)	....	39. (*look*)	....
15. (future)	....	40. (masculine)	....
16. (*read*)	....	41. (ána future)	....
17. (lāzim)	....	42. (híyya)	....
18. (positive)	....	43. (ínta)	....
19. (húwwa)	....	44. (perfect)	....
20. (3āyiz)	....	45. (ána)	....
21. (híyya)	....	46. (híyya)	....
22. (ínti)	....	47. (*live*)	....
23. (perfect)	....	48. (ínta)	....
24. (negative)	....	49. (*write*)	....
25. (*forget*)	....	50. (húwwa)	....

2. Oral Translation.

1. I'm researching
2. she stole
3. we're thanking
4. he'll go
5. you (m.) cried
6. you (f.) didn't cry
7. I visited
8. I (f.) want to sleep
9. they won't love
10. I didn't put
11. she dreamed
12. she danced
13. you (pl.) intend to pay
14. he doesn't run
15. you (pl.) don't bring
16. she doesn't sweep
17. go (m.)!
18. play (f.)!

3. Dice Drills.

You want to continue oral translation drills until it becomes second nature, that is, until you can produce the correct conjugation without hesitation. To do this, you'll need a "random verb form generator". There are two methods of randomly generating verb forms. The first is the dice method. You will need three standard dice. Use blank stickers to label each side of the dice as follows, or photocopy this page onto sticker paper.*

die 1: persons	ána	íḥna íntu	ínta ínti	húwwa	híyya	húmma
die 2: positive/ negative	**+**	**+**	**+**	**-**	**-**	**-**
die 3: tenses	perfect	bare imper-fect	bi-imper-fect	future	perfect	bi-imper-fect
die 4: imperative and participles	masc.	masc.	fem.	fem.	plural	plural

Once the dice are ready, make a short list of the verbs you would like to practice. You can use the verb indexes starting on p. 120. You could even make flash cards with the ECA verb written on one side, and the English translation written on the other side, and then shuffle the cards in random order. To start the drill, choose a verb and then roll the first three dice. It is best to make the conjugation an oral drill, but you can also write the verb form on paper if you'd prefer. If you are not sure of your conjugation, check its corresponding verb table.

katábt

For example, you want to practice conjugating the verb **kátab**. The roll of the dice tells you to conjugate the **positive perfect** form for **ána**. You say **katábt**.

After conjugating the verb, you can reroll one die to practice the conjugation with another person or tense. Alternatively, you could reroll all three dice and/or move on to another card. The key is mix it up and keep yourself on your toes.

The fourth die is used together with the second die for conjugating imperative forms in the positive and negative. The fourth die is used alone to practice conjugating either active or passive participles.

The second method is to use a grid as a substitute for dice. Several grids with different focuses are in Appendix B of in the back of *this* book. (Printable PDF versions are also available at www.lingualism.com/ecaverbs) Hold

---

* Printable stickers are also available as a PDF at www.lingualism.com/ecaverbs

a pen or pencil in hand, look away from the grid, and touch down with the pen(cil) tip somewhere randomly on the grid.

Example: **rāḥ** *to go*

In the example, the pen tip has landed on **ínta bi-imperfect**. You say:

bitrūḥ

Mabrūk! Congratulations!

You have completed parts 1, 2, and 3, which cover all forms of measure I verbs. There are twelve more measures, but you've already done more than half the work. How? You are now familiar with the prefixes and suffixes that you will continue to see in non-measure I verbs. You are also familiar with the rules for vowel changes that take place during conjugation. All that remains is to apply the same rules for conjugation to other verb patterns.

Part 4: Non-Measure I Verbs

Section 1: An Overview of Non-Measure I Verbs

1. Look at the verb tables for sound non-measure I verbs to determine which table each of the following verbs belongs to.

istáɣrab	ʃáxxar	istilá??af	ixtálaf
ʃánkil	itɣásal	sā3id	?ánqaz
itgáwwiz	istáħmil	dáħrag	isti?ákkid
infátaħ	istibārik	iswádd	
dárris	itfárrag	itgāwib	

1. 2s1 ....
2. 2s2 ....
3. 3s ....
4. 4s ....
5. 5s1 ....
6. 5s2 ....

7. 6s ....
8. 7s1 ....
9. 7s2 ....
10. 8s1 ....
11. 9s ....
12. 10s1 ....

13. 10s2 ....
14. 10.2s1 ....
15. 10.2s2 ....
16. 10.3s ....
17. 11s1 ....
18. 11s2 ....

2. As you can see from exercise 1, each measure has a distinct pattern of consonants and vowels. Below, the consonants of individual verbs have been replaced with C; consonants which are part of the measure's pattern have not. Determine which table each pattern belongs to.

1. itCáCCiC   ....
2. istáCCaC   ....
3. ?áCCaC   ....
4. iCCáCC   ....
5. CāCiC   ....
6. itCāCiC   ....
7. inCáCaC   ....
8. istiCáCCiC   ....

3. Without consulting the book, use your knowledge of non-measure I verb patterns to determine which table the following non-sound verbs belong to.

2d	4g	7h1	8h
3d	6d	8g	10d

1. ɣánna   ....
2. itlā?a   ....
3. ihtámm   ....
4. irtāħ   ....
5. nāda   ....
6. itgāb   ....
7. istá3na   ....
8. ?aṣárr   ....

Section 2: Measure II Verbs

1. Use your knowledge of conjugation to match the following verbs to their translations.

1. gáhhiz	I lent
2. kammílit	we killed
3. mawwítna	she completed
4. masabbitūʃ	he prepared
5. sallíft	they didn't stabilize
6. masallímtiʃ	you (m.) didn't greet
7. ʂammímti	I guess
8. baxámmin	he will teach
9. ħay3állim	she coaches
10. bitdárrab	(m.) don't smoke!
11. matdaxxánʃ	he doesn't move
12. mabiyħarrákʃ	he won't stop
13. miʃ ħatnádḍaf	you (m.) won't clean
14. miqarrarīn	(pl.) sing!
15. mabasárraħ	(pl.) deciding
16. maʂaħħáħtiʃ	you (f.) insisted
17. miʃ ħaywáʔʔaf	you (pl.) thought
18. bitxaṭṭáṭtu	(m.) show!
19. fakkártu	I didn't correct
20. ɣánnu	I'm not brushing
21. mádḍu	she didn't name
22. masammítʃ	we pray
23. binʂalli	you (pl.) are planning
24. warri	they spent

2. Change the following verbs in the perfect tense to the bi-imperfect, and the bi-imperfect tense to the perfect.

1. fákkar	....	5. bitɣánnu	....
2. kammílit	....	6. mádḍa	....
3. ba3állim	....	7. sallíft	....
4. biywárri	....	8. darrábna	....

3. Translate your answers from exercise 2 using the present simple or present continuous tense of English.

1.	3.	5.	7. ....
2.	4.	6.	8. ....

4. Make the following perfect and bi-imperfect verbs negative.

1. xámmin	....	5. gahhízna	....
2. sámma	....	6. mawwítt	....
3. ba3állim	....	7. bitqarráru	....
4. biyʂámmim	....	8. biyħarráku	....

5. Translate the following.

1. I smoked ....
2. it (m.) is stabilizing ....
3. we will pray ....
4. I (f.) want to show ....
5. he intends to stop ....
6. you (pl.) killed ....
7. she trained ....
8. I won't guess ....
9. he isn't teaching ....
10. you (m.) complete ....

11. you (f.) greeted ....
12. he didn't brush ....
13. we need to decide ....
14. you (pl.) mustn't smoke ....
15. he plans ....
16. you insist / she insists ....
17. you (f.) didn't correct ....
18. she's singing ....
19. they're not moving ....
20. I'm cleaning ....

6. Look at the verb index on p. 130-133 and the imperative forms in tables 2s1-2d to translate the following as if you were speaking to one man, one woman, and a group of people.

1. Teach! ....
2. Don't clean! ....
3. Pray! ....
4. Don't show! ....

7. Study the participles in verb tables 2s1-2d. Notice that the active and passive forms are identical. Then complete the following table with forms of the participle.

	gáhhiz	qárrar	wárra
masc.			
fem.			
plural			

8. Dice Drill! Choose two or three new verbs from each of the verb tables 2s1-2d. Then get out those conjugation dice or grids and continue drilling until you are comfortable producing the forms without hesitation. After you say each form out loud, think of the English translation.

Example: ʃáxxar *to snore*

mabyiʃaxxárʃ
he doesn't snore

Section 3: Measure III Verbs

1. Look at the verb index on p. 133-134 and translate the following verbs.

1. ʔābil	....	6. sāfir	....
2. fāgiʔ	....	7. zākir	....
3. gāwib	....	8. dāwa	....
4. ħāwil	....	9. fāda	....
5. sā3id	....	10. nāda	....

2. Translate the following perfect verbs.

1. ʔáblu	....	5. zákrit	....
2. gáwbit	....	6. dāwu	....
3. ħawílt	....	7. fadētu	....
4. safírna	....	8. nadēna	....

3. Make the following perfect verbs positive.

1. maʔablūʃ	....	4. manadítʃ	....
2. madawāʃ	....	5. maħawiltūʃ	....
3. mazakirtīʃ	....	6. maʔabíltiʃ	....

4. Translate the following bare imperfect, bi-imperfect, and future tense verbs.

1. 3āyiz asā3id	....	11. bitfādi	....
2. lāzim nigāwib	....	12. bitsā3id	....
3. basā3id	....	13. mabitsa3ídʃ	....
4. bingāwib	....	14. bitsá3di	....
5. lāzim maysafírʃ	....	15. mabitsa3dīʃ	....
6. mabiysafírʃ	....	16. miʃ ħayħāwil	....
7. ħaysāfir	....	17. mabiysafírʃ	....
8. biydāwi	....	18. 3áyza tʔábli	....
9. mabiydawīʃ	....	19. 3āyiz tiʔābil	....
10. bitfādu	....	20. lāzim matʔablīʃ	....

5. Translate the following.

1. I didn't meet	....	6. you (f.) need to answer	....
2. I don't meet	....	7. you (m.) need to answer	....
3. she helped	....	8. they'll try	....
4. he helped	....	9. they'll study	....
5. you (f.) answer	....	10. they aren't studying	....

6. Translate the following imperative forms.

1. (m.) Cure! ....
2. (f.) Study! ....
3. (pl.) Help! ....
4. (m.) Try! ....
5. (m.) Don't avoid! ....

6. (f.) Don't avoid! ....
7. (pl.) Don't travel! ....
8. (pl.) Travel! ....
9. (pl.) Don't call! ....
10. (f.) Answer! ....

7. Translate the following verbs with the active participle. Notice that the the participle prefix mi- assmiliates to m- because it is preceded by a vowel (the -a in the preceding word líssa).

1. ána líssa mzākir ....
2. íħna líssa mʔablīn ....
3. híyya líssa mnadíyya ....

4. they just cured ....
5. you (m.) just helped ....
6. I (f.) just studied ....

8. Dice Drill! You know what to do.

Section 4: Measure IV Verbs

Measure IV verbs are actually borrowings from Modern Standard Arabic. They are not very common in ECA and are mostly used in more formal language.

1. Complete the table by writing in the vowels which are found in tables 4s-4g. 'C' stands for consonant and represents the radicals. Mark the stressed syllable.

table	perfect húwwa form	imperfect húwwa form
4s	ʔ.....CC.....C	y.....CC.....C
4h	ʔ.....C.....C	y.....C.....C
4d	ʔ.....CC.....	y.....CC.....
4g	ʔ.....C.....CC	y.....C.....CC

2. Use the verb index on p. 134 to translate the following.

1. ʔasbátit ....
2. ʔa3lánu ....
3. ʔatáħti ....

4. ʔálɣit ....
5. ʔanhēna ....
6. ʔa3addēt ....

3. Translate the following.

1. maʔanhāʃ ....
2. ʔa3lánt ....
3. biyí3lin ....
4. mabyi3línʃ ....
5. lāzim ti3ídd ....

6. lāzim ti3íddi ....
7. maʔalɣūʃ ....
8. binísbit ....
9. ħatínhi ....
10. lāzim mayi3linūʃ ....

4. Chain Transformation Drill.

ʔá3lan

1. (ána) .... 4. (bi-imperfect).........................
2. (negative) .... 5. (finish) ....
3. (ínta) .... 6. (ínti) ....
7. (íntu) .... 14. (perfect) ....
8. (positive) .... 15. (prepare) ....
9. (future) .... 16. (positive) ....
10. (ána) .... 17. (híyya) ....
11. (permit) .... 18. (bi-imperfect) ....
12. (bi-imperfect) .... 19. (prove) ....
13. (negative) .... 20. (húmma) ....

5. Translate the following imperative forms.

1. (m.) Announce! .... 6. (m./f.) Don't finish! ....
2. (f.) Announce! .... 7. (pl.) Permit! ....
3. (m./f.) Finish! .... 8. (pl.) Don't permit! ....
4. (pl.) Finish! .... 9. (m./f.) Cancel! ....
5. (m.) Don't announce! .... 10. (f.) Don't prepare! ....

6. Translate the following verbs with the active participle. Notice that the the participle prefix is mu- instead of the more common mi-. After líssa, mu- assmiliates to m- only when this does not result in three adjacent consonants. Study the participles in the verb tables 4s-4g to determine which verbs this occurs in.

1. I (f.) just announced .... 4. we just prepared ....
2. Amīna just canceled .... 5. you (m.) just finished ....
3. Sa3īd just permitted .... 6. you (pl. just proved ....

7. The passive measure IV verb differs from its active participle form in its second vowel: i becomes a and ī becomes ā. Change the following active participles into passive participles.

1. mú3lin .... 4. mu3ídd ....
2. mutīħa .... 5. múɣli ....
3. munhiyīn .... 6. muɣlíyya ....

Take a few minutes to study the forms of passive measure IV verbs on p. 45. Such passive forms are not commonly used in ECA, and when they are, they are most often in the third person with an inanimate subject. Therefore, only the third person singular forms are shown. Of course, you can use your knowledge of conjugation to create other forms, as well. Compare the passive forms to their active counterparts and notice the difference in voweling. The pattern is quite straightforward.

8. Make the following active verbs passive.

1. ʔá3lan .... 4. ʔálqa ....
2. ʔaẓhárit .... 5. ʔaṣárr ....
3. ʔasār .... 6. ʔálɣu ....

9. Use the verb index on p. 134 to translate your answers from exercise 8.

1. .... 3. .... 5. ....
2. .... 4. .... 6. ....

10. Translate the following.

1. maʔu3línʃ ....
2. maʔulɣīʃ ....
3. biyúsbat ....
4. biyúlɣa ....
5. lāzim yutāħ ....

6. it mustn't be permitted ....
7. it (f.) will be canceled ....
8. it is (being) prepared ....
9. it isn't (being) prepared ....
10. it wasn't carried out ....

11. Wordsearch: Find correctly conjugated forms of the following verbs in the wordsearch puzzle and write them below along with their translations. Look at the verb index on p. 134 to find the meaning of new words. Be careful to avoid incorrect forms.

1. ʔághaɖ	4. ʔánha	7. ʔánqaz
2. ʔasār	5. ʔa3ádd	8. ʔatāħ
3. ʔálɣa	6. ʔá3dam	9. ʔásbat

```
ʔ  á  g  h  a  d  u  w  t  ī  ħ  x  m  u  3  ī  m
w  a  n  a  m  3  i  t  ṣ  ṭ  ʃ  m  a  b  ī  ħ  a
a  ħ  g  u  u  l  ʔ  ú  3  d  i  m  ʔ  n  ʃ  a  b
r  ɣ  ā  h  s  u  ī  ʔ  ā  í  ʐ  b  u  a  f  t  y
t  a  m  ʔ  á  ī  f  h  ʃ  á  m  g  l  t  ā  i  i
b  ī  a  r  r  d  3  m  a  ʔ  u  l  ɣ  ī  ʃ  n  s
u  s  ʔ  a  r  í  i  l  m  h  s  l  ā  ʃ  s  q  b
ʔ  i  m  u  d  ɣ  a  t  u  a  ā  l  ʃ  t  b  í  í
n  m  a  ʔ  a  n  h  í  t  ʃ  r  ʔ  x  ī  a  z  t
m  ā  h  ū  z  s  ī  n  ʔ  u  ɖ  i  u  f  3  u  ʃ
a  n  ē  t  ʃ  ú  m  a  3  d  á  m  t  u  d  ī  ú
m  a  t  i  n  q  í  z  t  u  l  ɣ  á  ī  a  á  ʔ
u  ʔ  ʃ  t  h  á  x  ʔ  a  3  á  d  d  t  ħ  m  z
```

1. ....
2. ....
3. ....
4. ....
5. ....
6. ....
7. ....
8. ....
9. ....

Section 5: Measure V Verbs

Compare the forms and meanings of the following measure II and measure V verbs.

measure II		measure V	
kámmil	complete	itkámmil	be completed
náḍḍaf	clean	itnáḍḍaf	be cleaned, become clean
gáhhiz	prepare	itgáhhiz	get ready
ḥárrak	move (something)	itḥárrak	move (around)
3állim	teach	it3állim	learn
xárrag	make (someone) exit	itxárrag	graduate (from university)

Measure V verbs act as the passive forms of measure II verbs, as seen in the first two examples. They can also act as non-transitive forms, as seen in the third and fourth examples. The last two examples show how measure V verbs can be used more idiomatically. Their meanings are not as predictable, although they are usually related to the meaning of their measure II counterparts. **it3állim** can mean *be taught*, but it usually means *learn*, which is a transitive verb, also. (*A transitive verb can take an object, while an intransitive verb cannot. In English, a single verb may be transitive an intransitive. For example, *He broke the plate.* and *The plate broke.* In ECA, however, a distinct verb is normally used for each meaning.)

1. Write the following form II verbs as their passive form V equivalents along with their translations.

1. sábbit   stabilize   ....
2. dárrab   coach   ....
3. ṣaḥḥaḥ   correct   ....
4. 3áyyid   celebrate   ....
5. sámma   name   ....

2. Use your knowledge of conjugation to match the following verbs to their translations.

1. itʔákkid   I speak
2. itgawwízu   he was certain
3. batkállim   she'll be appointed
4. lāzim tit3áwwid   they got married
5. ḥatit3áyyin   you (m.) need to get accustomed
6. itʔaxxártu   she just ate dinner
7. matfarrágtiʃ   you (pl.) were late
8. 3ayzīn nitṭállaʔ   he didn't eat lunch
9. matɣaddāʃ   I didn't watch
10. líssa mit3aʃʃíyya   we want to get divorced

3. Translate the following.

1. 3āyiz yitkállim   ....   7. biyitʔákkid   ....
2. lāzim nitɣádda   ....   8. itṭalláʔit   ....
3. bat3állim   ....   9. it3allímna   ....
4. miʃ 3áyza titfárrag ....   10. itḥarráktu   ....
5. it3aʃʃēt   ....   11. biyitgáhhiz   ....
6. mat3aʃʃítʃ   ....   12. 3ayzīn yitgawwízu ....

13. líssamitxarragīn	....	17. itkallími	....
14. mabyitgahhízʃ	....	18. itkállim	....
15. itnaḍḍáfit	....	19. biyit3áyyid	....
16. miʃ ḥatit3allímu	....	20. mat3ayyinūʃ	....

4. Chain Transformation Drill.

it3állim

1. (ána)	....	11. (bi-imperfect)	....
2. (híyya)	....	12. (húmma)	....
3. (*eat lunch*)	....	13. (positive)	....
4. (negative)	....	14. (perfect)	....
5. (ána)	....	15. (íḥna)	....
6. (positive)	....	16. (*be named*)	....
7. (ínta)	....	17. (negative)	....
8. (negative)	....	18. (bi-imperfect)	....
9. (future)	....	19. (húwwa)	....
10. (*watch*)	....	20. (ínti)	....

Section 6: Measure VI Verbs

Compare the forms and meanings of the following measure III and measure VI verbs.

measure III		measure VI	
gāwib	answer	itgāwib	be answered
dāra	hide	itdāra	be hidden
dāyiʔ	annoy	itdāyiʔ	be annoyed
ʔābil	meet	itʔābil	meet each other
sābiʔ	compete	itsābiʔ	compete with each other
-	-	it3āma	pretend to be blind
-	-	itmāriḍ	play sick

Measure VI verbs act as the passive forms of measure III verbs, as seen in the first three examples. They can also take on a reciprocal meaning, translating with *each other* and taking a plural subject, as seen in the fourth and fifth examples. The last two examples show how measure VI verbs can be used more idiomatically, often expressing that the subject is feigning a condition. Their meanings are not always predictable, although they are usually related to the meaning of their measure III counterparts.

1. Use the verb index on p. 136-137 to translate the following verbs. Notice that ā may shorten to a, and i may elide.

1. itʔáblu	....	8. itmaríḍt	....
2. matʔablūʃ	....	9. itmárḍit	....
3. batdāyiʔ	....	10. matmaríḍtiʃ	....
4. itdārit	....	11. matmardítʃ	....
5. itsámḥu	....	12. it3ámtu	....
6. matsámḥūʃ	....	13. líssamitgāwib	....
7. biyitsámḥu	....	14. ḥanit3āmil	....

15. itsábʔu	....	18. lāzim nitsāmiħ	....
16. miʃ 3áyza -tdāyiʔ	....	19. bititnákfu	....
17. mabtitʔablūʃ	....	20. matlaʔítʃ	....

2. Dice Drill!

Section 7: Measure VII Verbs

Compare the forms and meanings of the following measure I and measure VII verbs.

measure I		measure VII	
mísik	catch, arrest	itmásak	get caught, get arrested
ɣásal	wash	itɣásal	be washed
ɣāz	annoy	itɣāz	be annoyed
wílid	give birth	itwálad	be born
nísi	forget	itnása	be forgotten

Measure VII verbs act as the passive forms of measure I verbs. Regardless of the voweling of the measure I verb, the voweling of the measure VII perfect tense verb is itCáCaC, itCāC, itCáCa, itCáCC.

1. Translate the following perfect tense verbs using the verb index on p. 136-137 and the verb tables 7s1, 7h1, 7d1, and 7g1.

1. itkátab	....	5. matɣázʃ	....
2. itnasētu	....	6. matsaráʔʃ	....
3. itwaládt	....	7. itħábbu	....
4. itd́árru	....	8. matnasāʃ	....

2. Translate the following bare imperfect, bi-imperfect, and future tense verbs.

1. biyitkítib	....	5. nāwi yitmísik	....
2. ħayitwílid	....	6. bititṭíbix	....
3. 3āyiz atħább	....	7. biyitd́árr	....
4. binitɣāz	....	8. ħatnísi	....

3. Change the verbs in exercise 1 to the bi-imperfect.

1.	3.	5.	7. ....
2.	4.	6.	8. ....

4. Make the verbs in exercise 2 negative.

1.	3.	5.	7. ....
2.	4.	6.	8. ....

A second variety of measure VII verbs uses the prefix **in-** istead of **it-**. While the prefix **it-** is productive, that is, it can be added to create the passive form of any transitive measure I verb, the prefix **in-** is more idiomatic. Although it often also creates an alternative passive form of a measure I verb, it may also create an intransitive verb.

measure I		measure VII	
kátab	write	inkátab	be written
bā3	sell	inbā3	be sold
ball	moisten	inbáll	get wet
ḥána	bend	inḥána	bow

5. Translate the following 7s2, 7h2, 7d2, and 7g2 verbs.

1. inkátabit ....
2. mankatabítʃ ....
3. inḥanēt ....
4. inballēna ....
5. biyinfítiḥ ....
6. bitinbā3 ....
7. mabtinbá3ʃ ....
8. miʃ 3āyiz yinbáll ....
9. manḥanítʃ ....
10. manḥantīʃ ....

11. it (f.) will be written ....
12. it (m.) was sold ....
13. it (m.) will open ....
14. he is being hit ....
15. he's not being hit ....
16. it (f.) was bought ....
17. it (f.) is being solved ....
18. it (f.) needs to be sold ....
19. (f.) be quiet! ....
20. don't (pl.) be annoyed ....

Section 8: Measure VIII Verbs

1. Use your knowledge of conjugation to match the following verbs to their translations.

1. lāzim aftíkir	I need to remember
2. biyiʃtáɣal	she needs
3. bitiħtāg	he's working
4. irtāħu	they relaxed
5. biyihtámmu	they want to occupy
6. iʃtarētu	they are interested
7. intáha	they just borrowed
8. 3ayzīn yiħtállu	they didn't suggest
9. líssa mibtidi	you (pl.) bought
10. ħatixtāri	you (f.) will choose
11. iħtírmu	you (pl.) receive
12. iħtírim	it (m.) ended
13. iktaʃáfna	it just began
14. mabtintiqidʃ	it didn't differ
15. maxtaláfʃ	it (f.) united
16. líssa mistilfīn	(m.) respect!
17. ittáħadit	(f.) don't criticize
18. matintiqdīʃ	(pl.) respect!
19. maqtaraħūʃ	we discovered
20. bitistílmu	she doesn't complain

2. Circle the words to complete the following sentences.

Measure VIII verbs are formed by sandwiching the first radical with (1. i and t / i and n / is and t). The vowels of sound verbs in the perfect tense are (2. a / i / u), and become (3. a / i / u) in non-perfect tenses, except for the verb (4. iħtáram / iʃtáɣal / intáqad), which would be (5. yiħtírim / yiɣtáɣal / yintúqud) in the bare imperfect.

3. Translate the following.

1. mabaftikírʃ	....	11. it (m.) ended	....
2. ħaʃtáɣal	....	12. it (m.) didn't end	....
3. batiħtāg	....	13. it (f.) didn't unite	....
4. irtáħt	....	14. I'm choosing	....
5. istálamu	....	15. I'm not choosing	....
6. intáhit	....	16. you (pl.) differ	....
7. mantahítʃ	....	17. we'll suggest	....
8. miʃ 3āyiz aʃtíri	....	18. he doesn't complain	....
9. ihtámmi	....	19. (m.) choosing	....
10. iktáʃafu	....	20. (m.) chosen	....

4. Dice Drill!

5. Study the verb tables for passive measure VIII verbs on p. 64. Then translate the following.

1. he was respected ....
2. they were chosen ....
3. it (f.) will be bought ....
4. it (m.) was occupied ....

5. it (f.) was discovered ....
6. they were hunted ....
7. it (m.) wasn't recommended ....
8. I'm criticized ....

6. Make the following active verbs passive, and then translate your answer.

1. ħayiħtírim ....
2. iħtállit ....
3. istálam ....

4. intáxabu ....
5. mabyistilímʃ ....
6. lāzim tixtíṣir ....

Section 9: Measure IX Verbs

1. Translate the following.

1. iħmarrēti ....
2. biyiṣlí33 ....
3. maxḍárriʃ ....

4. ma3warrítʃ ....
5. 3ayzīn nismírr ....
6. ħayibyíḍḍ ....

2. Change the following perfect tense verbs to the bi-imperfect.

1. ibyáḍḍit ....
2. iwħáʃʃ ....
3. izrá?? ....

4. iħwallēt ....
5. iṣla33ēna ....
6. ismárru ....

3. Make your answers from exercise 2 negative, and then translate your answer.

1. ....
2. ....

3. ....
4. ....

5. ....
6. ....

4. Dice Drill!

Section 10: Measure X Verbs

1. Like measure II and measure V verbs, some measure verbs contain i in the final syllable (before suffixes) and some contain a. Translate the following sound verbs.

1. istaxdímit ....
2. mastaxdimítʃ ....
3. mastaxdímtiʃ ....
4. istaxdímti ....
5. biyistáxdim ....
6. mabyistaxdímʃ ....
7. ħastáxdim ....
8. 3āyiz tistáxdim ....
9. mabyistaxdimūʃ ....
10. istaxdímu ....

11. miʃ musta3ídd yistáħmil ....
12. húmma líssa mista3milīn ....
13. lāzim nistá3gil ....
14. istalṭáft ....
15. bitistamtá3u ....
16. mastarxáṣtiʃ ....
17. ħatistaɣrábi ....
18. mabastamtá3ʃ ....
19. lāzim matista3gílʃ ....
20. 3áli byistí3mil ....

2. Translate the following hollow verbs.

1. istaʔāl .... 5. mabtistagíbʃ ....
2. istafādu .... 6. lāzim matistahnīʃ ....
3. ʒāyiz astagīb .... 7. ħatistafīdu ....
4. binistaʔīl .... 8. istahān ....

3. Translate the following defective and geminate verbs.

1. istadfēt .... 5. ħayistamírr ....
2. istákfit .... 6. istaħaʔʔēti ....
3. istafázzu .... 7. biyistalázz ....
4. mabyistafizzūʃ .... 8. mabastalázziʃ ....

4. Dice Drill with sound measure X+II and measure X+III verbs.

Section 11: Measure X + II Verbs and Measure X + III Verbs

ECA has a few *hybrid* verbs which take the measure X **ist-** prefix and combine them with verbs which have the same patterns as measure II or III verbs.

1. Make the following perfect tense verbs negative, and then translate your answers.

1. istiʔákkid .... 5. istaláʔʔa ....
2. istiláʔʔaf .... 6. istánnit ....
3. istirayyáħit .... 7. istibárku ....
4. istaħámmu .... 8. istahílt ....

2. Change the verbs in exercise 1 to the positive bi-imperfect.

1. .... 5. ....
2. .... 6. ....
3. .... 7. ....
4. .... 8. ....

3. Dice Drill with non-sound measure X+II and measure X+III verbs.

Section 12: Measure XI Verbs

In part I, section 2, you learned that verbs have three radicals. All verb measures and forms we have encountered so far are based on three radicals, even if one of the radicals may not always be obvious (due to assimilation and elision). Measure XI verbs, on the other hand, have four radicals.

1. Translate the following.

1. dárdiʃ .... 5. dáħrag ....
2. farmílit .... 6. kahrábu ....
3. ʃankílt .... 7. laxbáțti ....
4. targímu .... 8. sayțárna ....

2. Make the verbs in exercise 1 negative.

1. .... 3. .... 5. .... 7. ....
2. .... 4. .... 6. .... 8. ....

3. Make the verbs in exercise 1 positive bi-imperfect.

1. .... 3. .... 5. .... 7. ....
2. .... 4. .... 6. .... 8. ....

4. Change your answers from exercise 3 into the negative bi-imperfect.

1. .... 3. .... 5. .... 7. ....
2. .... 4. .... 6. .... 8. ....

5. Chain Transformation Drill.

	tárgim		
1. (ána)	....	11. (negative)	....
2. (negative)	....	12. (*brake*)	....
3. (híyya)	....	13. (bi-imperfect)	....
4. (future)	....	14. (positive)	....
5. (húwwa)	....	15. (húmma)	....
6. (*occupy*)	....	16. (perfect)	....
7. (bi-imperfect)	....	17. (participle)	....
8. (positive)	....	18. (híyya)	....
9. (íntu)	....	19. (*mix up*)	....
10. (imperative)	....	20. (imperfect)	....

Like measure V, VI and VII verbs, passive measure XI verbs form their passive by adding the prefix **it-**. This is sometimes translated as an intransitive verb in English.

measure XI		**passive measure XI**	
tárgim	translate	ittárgim	be written
ʃánkil	trip (transitive)	itʃánkil	trip (intransitive)

6. Translate the following.

1. itʃankílt   .... 5. ḥatitkáhrab   ....
2. ittargímit   .... 6. matitzaḥláʔʃ   ....
3. mattargimítʃ   .... 7. batwáɣwiʃ   ....
4. itnarfízna   .... 8. mabtitnarfizūʃ   ....

7. The verb iṭmaʔánn is irregular. Study its various forms on p.84 for a few minutes, and then translate the following.

1. iṭmaʔánnit   .... 5. (pl.) feel reassured!   ....
2. she didn't feel reassured   .... 6. 3āyiz aṭmaʔánn   ....
3. baṭmaʔánn   .... 7. we don't feel reassured   ....
4. you (m.) will feel reassured .... 8. iṭmaʔannēt   ....

Section 13: Irregular Verbs

There are six more verbs which do not fit into any of the other tables. They each have their own tables on p. 85-91. Study each table for a few minutes before completing its corresponding exercise(s) below.

1. Study table i1. Then translate the following.

1. gēt	....	5. bāgi	....
2. gih	....	6. bitīgi	....
3. gat	....	7. ḥayīgi	....
4. gum	....	8. áyz- āgi	....

2. Make the verbs in exercise 1 negative.

1.	3.	5.	7. ....
2.	4.	6.	8. ....

3. Translate the following. (See exercise 2.1.14 if you need to review the rule for verbs of motion.)

1. we didn't come	....	5. you (pl.) don't come	....
2. he comes	....	6. she's coming	....
3. he's coming	....	7. (m.) come!	....
4. they're not coming	....	8. (m./f.) don't come!	....

4. Study table i2. Then translate the following.

1. ídda	....	5. ḥayíddu	....
2. íddu	....	6. íddi	....
3. biyíddi	....	7. middíyya	....
4. bitíddi	....	8. 3āyiz áddi	....

5. Make the verbs in exercise 4 negative.

1.	3.	5.	7. ....
2.	4.	6.	8. ....

6. Oral Translation.

1. we didn't give	3. you (pl.) will give	5. she's giving	7. she didn't give
2. so that I don't give	4. (pl.) give!	6. you (m.) give	8. (m.) given

7. Study table i3. Then translate the following.

1. kalt	....	5. biyākul	....
2. kúlu	....	6. mabyakúlʃ	....
3. makalūʃ	....	7. ḥatākul	....
4. bākul	....	8. ḥatákli	....

8. The verb xad (take) is conjugated the same way as kal. Change the verbs in exercise 7 to xad. Then translate.

1. ....
2. ....
3. ....
4. ....

5. ....
6. ....
7. ....
8. ....

9. Translate the following.

1. we're eating ....
2. (m.) eat! ....
3. you (pl.) are eating ....
4. they don't eat ....
5. he didn't take ....

6. she took ....
7. (m.) don't take! ....
8. he wants to take ....
9. he just ate ....
10. (f.) taken ....

10. Study table i3p. Then translate the following.

1. ittākil ....
2. bitittāxid ....
3. lāzim yittākil ....
4. ḥayittáxdu ....

5. it (m.) isn't being taken ....
6. I was taken ....
7. you (pl.) will be eaten ....
8. it (f.) wasn't eaten ....

11. Study table i4. Then translate the following.

1. láʔit ....
2. bitlāʔi ....
3. ӡāyiz alāʔi ....
4. ḥaylāʔi ....
5. malaʔāʃ ....

6. (pl.) find! ....
7. we find ....
8. they mustn't find ....
9. he just found ....
10. (m.) found ....

12. Study table i5. If you check the verb index on p. 140, you'll see that two irregular verbs are represented by table i5. Then translate the following.

1. wiʔíft ....
2. ána wāʔif ....
3. báʔaf ....
4. wiʔӡu ....
5. mawiʔfūʃ ....

6. he fell ....
7. she's standing ....
8. (pl.) stand! ....
9. he falls ....
10. he doesn't stand ....

13. Study table i6. Then translate the following.

1. íddan ....
2. maddánʃ ....
3. lāzim yiddánu ....
4. ḥáddan ....

5. he just called to prayer ....
6. we call to prayer ....
7. she wants to call to prayer ....
8. (m.) don't call to prayer ....

14. Multiple choice. Choose the correct form.

1. you (f.) are standing   a. bitúʔafi   b. bitúʔfi   c. ínti wáʔfa   d. ínti waʔfíyya

2. they didn't come   a. magúmʃ   b. magūʃ   c. mabiygūʃ   d. magihūʃ

3. (m.) take!   a. xud   b. xad   c. kal   d. wāxid

4. he's giving   a. biyíddi   b. biyídda   c. biyídd   d. biyíddu

5. they just ate   a. húmma líssa kálu   b. húmma líssa yākul   c. húmma líssa waklīn

6. I found   a. laʔt   b. laʔēt   c. laʔīt   d. alāʔi

15. Dice Drill with all irregular verbs!

Section 14: Review of Non-Measure I Verbs

1. Change the following verbs from the perfect tense to the bi-imperfect tense.

1. xámmin   ....   5. dárdiʃ   ....
2. itgāwib   ....   6. istá3mil   ....
3. zākir   ....   7. inbáll   ....
4. ʔatāħ   ....   8. ixtálaf   ....

2. Make your answers from exercise 1 negative.

1. ....   3. ....   5. ....   7. ....
2. ....   4. ....   6. ....   8. ....

3. Conjugate the verbs in exercise 1 for híyya.

1. ....   3. ....   5. ....   7. ....
2. ....   4. ....   6. ....   8. ....

4. Oral Translation.

1. she was interested   5. I met   9. (f.) don't get angry   13. they suntanned
2. she is loved   6. you (m.) didn't travel   10. they didn't fall   14. I (f.) want to learn
3. we choose   7. she showed   11. she'll graduate   15. (pl.) come!
4. they're singing   8. I didn't come   12. I became annoyed   16. (pl.) don't come!

5. Dice Drill with any non-measure I verbs.

Part 5: Suffixed Pronouns

Just as a pronoun subject is expressed through prefixes and suffixes added to the verb, object pronouns are in the form of suffixes. These suffixes often cause predictable changes in the verb according to the rules of sound changes. (See p. 12-15 to review these rules.) As long you are comfortable with the rules of sound changes, suffixed pronouns pose no new challenge, except that they result in even longer and more complex verb forms which may trip up your tongue. It is, therefore, a good idea to do lots of drills until the forms roll off your tongue with little effort or conscious thought.

Section 1: Direct Object Pronoun Suffixes

1. Take a look on p. 94 at the direct object pronoun suffixes which follow verbs ending in a single consonant (C+). Then translate the following.

1. ʃakárni	....	5. ʃakárku	....
2. ʃáfna	....	6. ʃákaru	....
3. ʃákarak	....	7. ʃáfha	....
4. ʃāfik	....	8. ʃakárhum	....

Notice number 6 above. The **húwwa** form plus the direct object pronoun suffix **-u** has the same form as the **húmma** form without a direct object pronoun. There is rarely ambiguity, however, as context will make the meaning clear.

2. All of the verbs in exercise 1 are the húwwa form. Conjugate the same verbs for híyya. Note that the i in the suffix -it never elides. It is also an exception to the rules of word stress, as it takes the stress even when followed by a suffix beginning in a vowel. (See Third to Last Syllable on p. 12.)

1.	3.	5.	7. ....
2.	4.	6.	8. ....

3. Conjugate the same verbs for húmma. Notice that húmma verbs end in a vowel, which is lengthened before the suffixes. Some of the suffixes take a different form following a vowel.

1.	3.	5.	7. ....
2.	4.	6.	8. ....

4. Conjugate the same verbs for ána and ínta, which share a single form in the perfect tense. For sound and hollow verbs, like those in these exericises, the -t suffix creates a verb form ending in two consonants. A pronoun suffix beginning with a consonant would result in three adjacent consonants, and so a vowel is inserted. Study the CC+ suffixes on p. 94.

1.	3.	5.	7. ....
2.	4.	6.	8. ....

5. The subject and object of a verb cannot normally be the same for the first and second persons. That is, you cannot say 'I saw me' or 'you saw you'. As in English, Arabic would use a reflexive pronoun object; for example, 'I saw myself'. This limits the interpretation of some of the forms in exercise 4. Translate your answers from exercise 4.

1. .... 3. .... 5. .... 7. ....
2. .... 4. .... 6. .... 8. ....

6. Make your answers from exercise 2 negative. Notice that the negative -ʃ suffix follows the pronoun suffix and carries the word stress.

1. .... 3. .... 5. .... 7. ....
2. .... 4. .... 6. .... 8. ....

7. And now for the negative húmma form. Although the -u suffix seems to be elidible in some forms, it is often enunciated to avoid ambiguity with the húwwa form.

1. .... 3. .... 5. .... 7. ....
2. .... 4. .... 6. .... 8. ....

8. Do the same for the ána/ínta form.

1. .... 3. .... 5. .... 7. ....
2. .... 4. .... 6. .... 8. ....

For those of you who are still with us, a hearty **good job!** is in order. Take a few minutes to sweep up any hair you've pulled out while doing the last several exercises, clear your mind, and relax before moving on.

9. Add the húwwa direct object pronoun suffix (-u) to the following verbs, and then translate. Translate the suffix as him or it, depending on the context.

1. kátab   ....   5. 3āyiz azūr   ....
2. báktib   ....   6. bánu   ....
3. makasarítʃ   ....   7. iʃtára   ....
4. bitḥíbb   ....   8. makalnāʃ   ....

10. Change the direct object pronoun suffix in your answers from exercise 9 to the híyya suffix.

1. .... 3. .... 5. .... 7. ....
2. .... 4. .... 6. .... 8. ....

11. Translate the following.

1. they didn't see me   ....   8. they didn't study it (m.) ....
2. she killed him   ....   9. he healed you (f.)   ....
3. you (m.) will coach them ....   10. they don't understand me ....
4. we moved it (f.)   ....   11. I heard you (m.)   ....
5. I respect you (f.)   ....   12. I didn't hear you (m.) ....
6. I don't respect him   ....   13. I (m.) want to wear it (m.) ....
7. I opened it (m.)   ....   14. you (pl.) bought it (f.) ....
15. (m.) eat it (m.)   ....   28. you (f.) are singing it (m.) ....

16. (f.) eat it (m.) ....
17. I didn't say it (m.) ....
18. I won't eat it (m.) ....
19. you (f.) need to sell it (f.) ....
20. you (f.) mustn't sell it (f.) ....
21. you (m.) threw it (f.) ....
22. I forgot it (m.) ....
23. we forgot it (m.) ....
24. we didn't forget it (m.) ....
25. I'm putting it (f.) ....
26. you (pl.) are completing it (m.) ....
27. they helped me ....

29. you (pl.) are singing it (m.) ....
30. I didn't meet them ....
31. he just ate it (m.) ....
32. she just showed it (f.) ....
33. they choose me ....
34. you (f.) tripped me ....
35. he rolls it (f.) ....
36. they just wrote it (m.) ....
37. you (m.) aren't giving it (m.) ....
38. you (pl.) aren't giving it (f.) ....
39. he'll wait for us ....
40. he considers it to be too few ....

12. Dice Drill! *Not all verbs take direct objects, and some logically only (or usually) take inanimate objects. For example, buy can take the object it or them, but you are unlikely to ever need to say 'She bought you.' It makes more sense to practice such verbs with inanimate objects. Below are two lists. The first logically takes objects of all persons, while the second takes inanimate objects. Do dice drills for verbs from each list.*

List 1: objects of all persons	List 2: inanimate objects
lámas *touch*	bá3at *send*
rásam *draw*	gáma3 *collect*
fíhim *understand*	ɣásal *wash*
bās *kiss*	ʃírib *drink*
sāb *leave*	ʔāl *say*
ħabb *love*	ʔára *read*
gáhhiz *prepare*	ħaṭṭ *put*
fāgiʔ *surprise*	xáṭṭaṭ *plan*
intáxab *elect*	ʔá3lan *announce*
istáħmil *tolerate*	it3állim *learn*
istánna *wait for*	iʃtára *buy*
láxbaṭ *confuse*	kal *eat*

Section 2: Indirect Object Pronoun Suffixes

verbs which commonly take indirect objects	
ʔāl *say*	málla *dictate*
bá3at *send*	nāwil *hand*
gāb *bring*	sállif *lend*
kátab *write*	sállim *hand over*
ídda *give*	wárra *show*

Verbs which take indirect objects often also require a direct object. The following nouns will appear in the exercises in this section:

masculine nouns:	feminine nouns:
kitāb *book*	hidíyya *present, gift*
gawāb *letter*	ʔíṣṣa *story*
xábar *news*	3arabíyya *car*

The indirect object pronoun suffix is formed by inserting the consonant l before forms of the direct object pronoun suffix. A vowel is inserted when necessary to avoid three adjacent consonants. The direct object **-ni** becomes **-li**. Study the table on p. 95.

1. Translate the following short sentences. Each consists of a verb with an indirect object pronoun suffix and a direct object noun.

1. iddāli kitāb. ....
2. katabtíli gawāb. ....
3. katabtílak gawāb. ....
4. sallifítlu -l3arabíyya. ....

5. ʔultílhum ilxábar. ....
6. ħaygíblik hidíyya. ....
7. ħayiddālik hidíyya. ....
8. warritúlna -lgawāb. ....

2. Make the sentences in exercise 1 negative.

1. .... 3. .... 5. .... 7. ....
2. .... 4. .... 6. .... 8. ....

3. Make the sentences in exercise 1 positive bi-imperfect.

1. .... 3. .... 5. .... 7. ....
2. .... 4. .... 6. .... 8. ....

4. Make your answers from exercise 3 negative.

1. .... 3. .... 5. .... 7. ....
2. .... 4. .... 6. .... 8. ....

5. Translate the following.

1. She wrote a letter to me. ....
2. He's telling me a story. ....
3. They gave us a book. ....
4. (m./f.) Give them a book! ....
5. She's handing me a letter. ....
6. They lent me the book. ....
7. I'll bring you (pl.) a present. ....
8. He didn't dictate the story to me. ....
9. They didn't write to you (f.). ....
10. We're showing them the car. ....
11. You (f.) didn't hand the letter over to me. ....
12. You (m.) need to hand her the letter. ....
13. They want to send the letter to you (pl.). ....

14. I'll tell them the news.   ....

15. I didn't tell them the news.   ....

16. He isn't telling her a story.   ....

17. (m.) Send him a letter!   ....

18. I brought her a present.   ....

19. You (m.) handed over the car to us. ....

20. (m./f.) Don't give her the car.   ....

6. Dice drill! Use the verbs at the beginning of the section.

Section 3: Direct + Indirect Object Pronoun Suffixes

As seen in the exercises in the previous section, when a verb takes both a direct and indirect object, the direct object tends to be inanimate. The third-person singular (**húwwa**) direct object tends to begin with **h**. Study the table on p. 96.

1. Translate the following.

1. iddahūli.   ....   5. ʔultuhúlhum.   ....
2. katabtihūli.   ....   6. ḥaygíbhālik.   ....
3. katabtuhūlak.   ....   7. ḥayiddahālik.   ....
4. sallifithālu.   ....   8. warrituhúlna.   ....

2. Change the noun to a direct pronoun suffix preceding the indirect pronoun suffix in your translations from exercise 5 in section 2.

1. ....   11. ....
2. ....   12. ....
3. ....   13. ....
4. ....   14. ....
5. ....   15. ....
6. ....   16. ....
7. ....   17. ....
8. ....   18. ....
9. ....   19. ....
10. ....   20. ....

3. Dice drill!

Part 6: To Have and To Be

Section 1: To Be

The verb **kān** is conjugated in the same way as other 1h1 verbs, except that it is not normally expressed in the bi-imperfect. Instead, a simple subject precedes its predicate, which can be an adjective, a noun, or a location.

	ána ta3bāna.	I (f.) am tired.
Examples:	húwwa mudárris.	He's a teacher.
	ħāmid wi sálma fi -lbēt.	ħāmid and Salma are at home.

As you can see in the examples above, *am, is,* and *are* are not expressed. *He's a teacher* is literally *he teacher.* The negative is formed by inserting miʃ before the predicate.

	ána miʃ ta3bāna.	I (f.) am not tired.
Examples:	húwwa miʃ mudárris.	He isn't a teacher.
	ħāmid wi sálma miʃ fi -lbēt.	ħāmid and Salma aren't at home.

The following words and expressions will appear in the exercises in this section:

fōʔ ittarabēza *on the table*	gamīl, gamīla *handsome, beautiful*
fi -lmadrása *at school*	ga3ān, ga3āna *hungry*
fī maṣr *in Egypt*	hína *here*
3and idduktūr *at the doctor's*	ṭālib (m.), ṭálba (f.) *student*

1. Translate the following.

1. sámya ṭálba. ....
2. ána ga3ān. ....
3. ikkitāb fōʔ ittarabēza. ....
4. húwwa 3and idduktūr. ....
5. ilhidíyya fi -l3arabíyya. ....
6. ħussām wi xālid fī maṣr. ....
7. dīna gamīla. ....
8. íħna fi -lmadrása. ....

2. Oral transformation: Make the sentences in exercise 1 negative.

When expressing a time other than the present, a form of the verb **kān** is required. Compare the following:

húwwa hína.	He's here.
kān hína.	He was here.
ħaykūn hína.	He'll be here.
āyiz yikūn hína.	He want to be here.

Notice that the pronoun subject is required in the first example, but absent in the present of a verb, as is the usual case in Arabic.

3. Study the table on p. 102. Then change the sentences in exercise 1 to the perfect tense.

1. .... 3. .... 5. .... 7. ....
2. .... 4. .... 6. .... 8. ....

4. Oral transformation: Make your answers in exercise 3 negative.

5. Translate the following.

1. ḥásan wasn't here. ....
2. He intends to be at school. ....
3. The book is on the table. ....
4. You (f.) are hungry. ....
5. We're not in Egypt. ....
6. We weren't in Egypt. ....
7. The teacher is in the car. ....
8. Naṣr will be at the doctor's. ....
9. Húda wants to be beautiful. ....
10. The student (m.) mustn't be on (top of) the table. ....
11. ḥásan isn't here. ....
12. You (pl.) were at school. ....
13. The book was on the table. ....
14. You were hungry. ....
15. They're in Egypt. ....
16. They were in Egypt. ....
17. The teacher (f.) will be at school. ....
18. Naṣr wasn't at home. ....
19. Nabīl doesn't want to be in the car. ....
20. You (f.) weren't here. ....

6. Study Compound Tenses on p. 112. Then translate the following.

1. biyi3mílu ....
2. mabyi3milūʃ ....
3. kānu biyi3mílu ....
4. makanūʃ biyi3mílu ....
5. 3ámalu ....
6. ma3amalūʃ ....
7. kānu 3ámalu ....
8. makanūʃ 3ámalu ....
9. ḥayi3mílu ....
10. miʃ ḥayi3mílu ....
11. ḥaykūnu biyi3mílu ....
12. miʃ ḥaykūnu biyi3mílu ....
13. ḥaykūnu 3ámalu ....
14. miʃ ḥaykūnu 3ámalu ....
15. kānu ḥayi3mílu ....
16. makanūʃ ḥayi3mílu ....

7. Change the verb forms in exercise 6 to the first-person singular (ána) form using the verb bána.

1. ....
2. ....
3. ....
4. ....
5. ....
6. ....
7. ....
8. ....

9. ....
10. ....
11. ....
12. ....
13. ....
14. ....
15. ....
16. ....

8. Translate the following.

1. I was watching ....
2. I won't have finished ....
3. we were going to go ....
4. you (m.) will be watching ....
5. you (f.) had finished ....

6. you (pl.) had seen ....
7. you (pl.) hadn't seen ....
8. he'll have eaten ....
9. he was going to eat ....
10. she'll be living ....

9. Remember that verbs of motion and location require the active participle rather than the bi-imperfect. Translate the following.

1. kān rāyiḥ ....
2. kānit gáyya ....
3. ḥakūn wáʔfa ....
4. ḥatkūnu rayḥīn ....
5. makúntiʃ ʔā3id ....

6. he wasn't standing ....
7. you (pl.) will be coming ....
8. we're going ....
9. she wasn't going ....
10. they'll be sitting ....

Section 2: To Have

In addition to vocabulary introduced in previous sections and those used in the examples in the book, the following words will appear in the exercises in this section:

axx *brother*	ṣudā3 *headache*
máyya *water*	aṣḥāb *friends*
wallā3a *lighter*	ʔakl *food*
ʃánṭa *bag*	ʔōḍa *room*

1. Study p. 100-101. Notice that the possessive pronoun suffixes which are attached to the prepositions are identical to direct object pronoun suffixes, except for -i (instead of -ni). Then translate the following.

1. 3ándi ....
2. ma3andūʃ ....
3. 3andína ....
4. líyya ....

5. malūʃ ....
6. ma3andināʃ ....
7. ma3āk ....
8. līha ....

2. Translate the following sentences.

1. 3ándi 3arabíyya. ....
2. 3andáha ṣudā3. ....
3. līna axx. ....
4. li uxt. ....

5. ma3āya wallā3a. ....
6. ma3ā filūs. ....
7. 3andúhum bēt gamīl. ....
8. lu aṣḥāb. ....

3. Make the sentences in exercise 2 negative.

1. ....
2. ....

3. ....
4. ....

5. ....
6. ....

7. ....
8. ....

4. Translte the following sentences in various tenses.

1. kān 3ándi kitāb. ....
2. rīm kān 3andáha ṣudā3. ....
3. ilbēt ḥaykūn lu ʔōḍa kbīra. ....
4. iṭṭālib 3āyiz yikūn 3ándu 3arabíyya.
....

5. kān ma3āki gawāb. ....
6. kān ma3āna máyya. ....
7. sa3īd lu ax wi uxt. ....
8. ilmudárris ḥaykūn 3ándu ʔōḍa gamīla fi - lmadrása. ....

5. Make the sentences in exercise 4 negative.

1. ....
2. ....
3. ....
4. ....

5. ....
6. ....
7. ....
8. ....

6. Translate the following.

1. 3amr doesn't have friends. ....
2. The doctor had a big house. ....
3. I don't have food with me. ....
4. She has a beautiful bag. ....
5. Fawzíyya doesn't have a brother. ....
6. You (f.) have beautiful eyes. ....
7. How old is 3úmar? ....
8. I (m.) want to have a big room. ....
9. We didn't have a car. ....
10. Mágdi had a fever. ....

Part 7: Review By Tense

Write the following verbs and their translations in the table below.

ʔálya	dárdiʃ	ħílim	istaħámma	iʃtára	ixtār	sāʒid
ʔatāħ	gāb	ídda	istaħáʔʔ	itʒáwwid	kān	ʃáraħ
ʔaʒádd	gih	ihtámm	istálaf	itbāʒ	kátab	ṭār
ʔáʒlan	gíri	inbāʒ	istamárr	itnākif	náḍḍaf	xad
ʔāl	ɣánna	inbáll	istámtaʒ	itnása	nām	xāf
baṣṣ	ħabb	istádfa	istánna	itwálad	nísi	ʒállim
báʔa	ħāwil	istafād	iʃláʒʒ	itzáħlaʔ	ráma	

	sound	hollow	defective	geminate
measure I				
measure II				
measure III				
measure IV				
measure V				
measure VI				
measure VII				
measure VIII				
measure IX				
measure X				
measure X+II				
measure X + III				
measure XI				
measure XI passive				
irregular				

Section 1: Perfect Verbs

The following exercises contain verbs from various measures in the preceding table.

1. Translate the following sound and irregular verbs.

1. I explained ....
2. she dreamed ....
3. he didn't clean ....
4. we taught ....
5. they wrote ....
6. you (f.) helped ....
7. you (m.) didn't try ....
8. you (pl.) announced ....
9. she didn't get accustomed ....
10. they teased each other ....

11. you (m.) were born ....
12. I didn't borrow ....
13. I went bald ....
14. we enjoyed ....
15. you (f.) waited ....
16. they didn't chat ....
17. he slipped ....
18. you (f.) didn't give ....
19. I didn't come ....
20. we didn't take ....

2. Translate the following hollow verbs.

1. you (pl.) said ....
2. I wasn't ....
3. we brought ....
4. they flew ....
5. she didn't sleep ....
6. he wasn't afraid ....
7. you (m.) allowed ....
8. it (f.) was sold ....
9. you (pl.) chose ....
10. we didn't benefit ....

11. she didn't say ....
12. they were ....
13. you (f.) didn't bring ....
14. I didn't fly ....
15. you (m.) slept ....
16. we were afraid ....
17. they didn't allow ....
18. it (m.) wasn't sold ....
19. I didn't choose ....
20. you (f.) benefited ....

3. Translate the following defective verbs.

1. you (m.) became ....
2. I didn't throw ....
3. she forgot ....
4. they didn't run ....
5. he sang ....
6. we canceled ....
7. you (pl.) didn't buy ....
8. I felt warm ....
9. you (f.) bathed ....
10. it (f.) wasn't forgotten ....

11. he didn't become ....
12. we threw ....
13. they didn't forget ....
14. I ran ....
15. he didn't sing ....
16. you (f.) didn't cancel ....
17. she bought ....
18. you (m.) didn't feel warm ....
19. you (pl.) didn't bathe ....
20. it (m.) was forgotten ....

4. Translate the following geminate verbs.

1. I looked ....
2. we loved ....
3. you (m.) prepared ....
4. you (f.) didn't get wet ....
5. you (pl.) were interested ....
6. he didn't continue ....
7. she deserved ....

8. they didn't look ....
9. I didn't love ....
10. we didn't prepare ....
11. you (m.) got wet ....
12. he wasn't interested ....
13. you (f.) continued ....
14. I didn't deserve ....

5. Make the following verbs negative.

1. istamtá3u ....
2. gēti ....
3. iʂlá33 ....
4. kúnna ....
5. iʃtáru ....
6. ixtārit ....
7. nisīt ....
8. ħabb ....
9. kalt ....
10. ɣánnu ....

11. dardíʃna ....
12. gum ....
13. gih ....
14. rámit ....
15. ramēt ....
16. ramēti ....
17. ħílim ....
18. sá3du ....
19. istamárrēt ....
20. xúftu ....

6. Make the following verbs passive.

1. ʃáraħ ....
2. 3állim ....
3. ħábbit ....
4. ʔá3lanit ....

5. ʔatāħ ....
6. ʔāl ....
7. sá3dit ....
8. xad ....

7. Oral Chain Transformation Drill. Do not write your answers, but rather say them aloud.

gíri

1. (negative)
2. (híyya)
3. (positive)
4. (get wet)
5. (ána)

6. (húmma)
7. (negative)
8. (take)
9. (íħna)
10. (positive)

11. (íntu)
12. (say)
13. (húmma)
14. (negative)
15. (give)

16. (ínti)
17. (húwwa)
18. (positive)
19. (cancel)
20. (híyya)

Section 2: Bare Imperfect Verbs

1. Translate the following sound and irregular imperfect verbs.

1. I (m.) want to come ....
2. he might go bald ....
3. you (pl.) need to announce ....
4. they want to help ....
5. you (m./f.) might wait ....

6. I (f.) don't want to slip ....
7. so that she gives ....
8. so that we don't enjoy ....
9. you (m./f.) mustn't give ....
10. we don't need to explain ....

2. Translate the following hollow imperfect verbs.

1. you (pl.) want to say ....
2. he/it mustn't be ....
3. he doesn't want to choose ....
4. so that we're not afraid ....
5. she doesn't need to sleep ....
6. she wants to sleep ....
7. I need to bring ....
8. they might fly ....

3. Translate the following defective imperfect verbs.

1. they want to buy ....
2. it (m.) needs to be forgotten ....
3. you (m.) are willing to cancel ....
4. we don't need to become ....
5. you (pl.) are willing to forget ....
6. you (m./f.) might sing ....
7. you (pl.) mustn't run ....
8. so that you (m.) bathe ....

4. Translate the following geminate imperfect verbs.

1. I (m.) want to look ....
2. you mustn't get wet ....
3. I (f.) intend to continue ....
4. they might be interested ....
5. he doesn't need to prepare ....
6. so that she deserves ....

5. Make the following verbs negative.

1. áħlam ....
2. yitīħ ....
3. tiħāwil ....
4. yidardíʃu ....
5. tiħíbbi ....
6. tírmu ....
7. nistádfa ....
8. ti3állim ....

6. Make the following verbs passive.

1. yinádḍaf ....
2. tibī3 ....
3. yisā3id ....
4. yitīħ ....
5. tiħíbb ....
6. áwlid ....

7. Translate the following.

1. I (m.) don't want to dream ....
2. we like to tease each other ....
3. he likes to clean ....
4. she wants to throw ....
5. they need to bathe ....
6. you (f.) want to borrow ....
7. we might chat ....
8. I (f.) need to try ....
9. you (pl.) are willing to teach ....
10. you (m./f.) intend to come ....

Section 3: Bi-Imperfect Verbs

1. Translate the following sound and irregular bi-imperfect verbs.

1. you (m.) take ....
2. we give ....
3. they wait ....
4. he's going bald ....
5. they're getting used to (it) ....
6. I come ....
7. she's writing ....
8. he doesn't give ....
9. you (m.) announce ....
10. I don't announce ....
11. we don't take ....
12. they're chatting ....

74 Egyptian Colloquial Arabic Verbs Exercise Book

13. you (f.) slip ....
14. you (m.) don't enjoy ....
15. she isn't waiting ....
16. I borrow ....

17. they explain ....
18. you (pl.) don't explain ....
19. he doesn't clean ....
20. she isn't dreaming ....

2. Translate the following hollow bi-imperfect verbs.

1. you (pl.) benefit ....
2. they don't choose ....
3. she isn't afraid ....
4. I'm flying ....
5. we sleep ....
6. you (pl.) don't say ....
7. he's bringing ....
8. they allow ....
9. it (m.) isn't sold ....
10. I say ....

11. I'm not benefiting ....
12. you (f.) choose ....
13. we're afraid ....
14. It (m.) doesn't fly ....
15. you (pl.) aren't sleeping ....
16. they're saying ....
17. she doesn't bring ....
18. you (f.) don't allow ....
19. it (f.) is being sold ....
20. I'm afraid ....

3. Translate the following defective bi-imperfect verbs.

1. I'm buying ....
2. we don't run ....
3. you (m.) aren't forgotten ....
4. you (f.) don't forget ....
5. you (pl.) cancel ....
6. he sings ....
7. she's throwing ....
8. they're becoming ....
9. he's bathing ....
10. she doesn't feel warm ....

11. they're not buying ....
12. she runs ....
13. he is being forgotten ....
14. we forget ....
15. I'm not canceling ....
16. you (pl.) aren't singing ....
17. you (m.) don't throw ....
18. you (f.) don't become ....
19. they don't bathe ....
20. I feel warm ....

4. Translate the following geminate bi-imperfect verbs.

1. he looks ....
2. she's interested ....
3. I'm preparing ....
4. you (f.) love ....
5. you (pl.) continue ....
6. he's getting wet ....
7. you (f.) derserve ....

8. I don't look ....
9. they're not interested ....
10. she doesn't prepare ....
11. they don't get wet ....
12. you (m.) aren't continuing ....
13. I don't love ....
14. we don't deserve ....

5. Make the following verbs negative.

1. biyídris ....
2. biysáfru ....
3. binsárraḥ ....
4. bitxúʃʃ ....
5. biyzūr ....
6. biyíbdu ....

7. bitbī3i ....
8. biyīgi ....
9. bastiʔákkid ....
10. bitākul ....
11. bitnāmu ....
12. bitgību ....

13. biyiʃrábu	17. biylāʔi ....
14. biyímʃi	18. bitṣáḥḥaḥ ....
15. bitistirayyáḥi	19. biywárri ....
16. binityāz	20. bit3abbári ....

6. Make the following verbs passive.

1. biy3állim	5. bitixtār ....
2. biytīḥ	6. mabtiʃtirīʃ ....
3. biyíktib	7. mabtistaxdímʃ ....
4. bitínsa	8. biyākul ....

7. Translate the following.

1. I'm getting wet	8. he doesn't sing ....
2. You (m.) aren't helping	9. she forgets ....
3. they say	10. they teach ....
4. he doesn't choose	11. you (m.) look ....
5. we're not interested	12. you (pl.) are chatting ....
6. you (pl.) don't love	13. he becomes ....
7. he sings	14. we aren't flying ....

Section 4: Future Verbs

1. Translate the following sound and irregular imperfect verbs.

1. he'll explain	6. he won't go bald ....
2. you (m.) will take	7. she won't slip ....
3. I'll wait	8. we'll dream ....
4. they'll come	9. you (pl.) will announce ....
5. you (f.) will try	10. I won't give ....

2. Translate the following hollow imperfect verbs.

1. he'll bring	5. she'll be ....
2. they'll benefit	6. it (m.) will be sold ....
3. we'll allow	7. you (f.) won't be afraid ....
4. I won't say	8. you (m.) won't choose ....

3. Translate the following defective imperfect verbs.

1. she won't become	6. you (m./f.) will throw ....
2. we'll buy	7. I'll forget ....
3. they'll sing	8. you (pl.) will feel warm ....
4. we won't cancel	9. it (m.) will be forgotten ....
5. I won't run	10. he won't bathe ....

4. Translate the following geminate imperfect verbs.

1. you (pl.) will love	....	4. they'll look	....
2. we won't continue	....	5. he'll deserve	....
3. I'll prepare	....	6. she won't be interested	....

5. Make the following verbs negative.

1. ḥagīb	....	3. ḥanistánna	....
2. ḥayiktíbu	....	4. ḥatɣínni	....

6. Translate the following.

1. she won't explain	....	6. you (f.) will look	....
2. we'll come	....	7. you (m.) won't be	....
3. you (pl.) will forget	....	8. he'll chat	....
4. I won't be afraid	....	9. you (m.) will prepare	....
5. they'll continue	....	10. they won't eat	....

Section 5: Imperatives

1. Translate the following sound and irregular imperative verbs.

1. (pl.) Be quiet!	....	6. (f.) Don't explain!	....
2. (m.) Don't borrow!	....	7. (m.) Hit!	....
3. (f.) Come!	....	8. (f.) Help!	....
4. (m.) Take!	....	9. (f.) Write!	....
5. (pl.) Don't slip!	....	10. (pl.) Don't chat!	....

2. Translate the following hollow imperative verbs.

1. (m.) Sleep!	....	4. (m.) Bring!	....
2. (f.) Choose!	....	5. (f.) Don't be!	....
3. (pl.) Be!	....	6. (pl.) Don't be afraid!	....

3. Translate the following defective imperative verbs.

1. (m./f.) Run!	....	4. (pl.) Bathe!	....
2. (m.) Become!	....	5. (m.) Don't forget!	....
3. (f.) Become!	....	6. (pl.) Don't sing!	....

4. Translate the following geminate imperative verbs.

1. (m.) Don't look!	....	4. (pl.) Don't continue!	....
2. (f.) Be interested!	....	5. (f.) Don't get wet!	....
3. (pl.) Love!	....	6. (m.) Prepare!	....

5. Make the following verbs negative.

1. ta3āla   ....
2. hātu   ....
3. iktíbi   ....

4. ʔābil   ....
5. ʔūlu   ....
6. ígri   ....

Section 6: Participles

1. Translate the following active participles.

1. (m.) explaining   ....
2. (f.) exiting   ....
3. (pl.) giving birth   ....
4. (m.) kissing   ....
5. (f.) throwing   ....
6. (pl.) believing   ....

7. (m.) teaching   ....
8. (f.) showing   ....
9. (pl.) meeting   ....
10. (m.) announcing   ....
11. (f.) coming   ....
12. (pl.) taking   ....

2. The active participle fākir translates as remember. Translate the following.

1. ínta fakírni?   ....
2. ána fakrāk.   ....
3. ána fakírki.   ....

4. íntu fakrínna?   ....
5. ána miʃ fákru.   ....
6. ána miʃ fakrā.   ....

3. Translate the following.

1. Do you (m.) remember us? ....
2. I (m.) don't remember her. ....
3. I (f.) don't remember her. ....

4. They remember him. ....
5. They remember her. ....
6. She remembers you (pl.). ....

4. Dice Drill ad infinitum!

Mabrūk!

You've finished all the exercises in this book. You should, at this point, feel comfortable with ECA verbs and their conjugation patterns, especially when it comes to the sound changes that occur when prefixes and suffixes are added. You won't have mastered ECA verbs yet. This will take continued commitment, effort, and drills, drills, drills. Best wishes for success in your learning!

1.1.1. 1. ána 2. íḥna 3. ínta 4. ínti 5. íntu 6. húwwa 7. híyya 8. húmma

1.1.2. 1. ána 2. íḥna 3. ínta 4. ínti 5. íntu 6. íntu 7. íntu 8. húwwa 9. híyya 10. húmma 11. húmma 12. húmma 13. húmma

1.2.1. 1. kátab 2. húwwa (third-person masculine singular), perfect tense

1.2.2. 1. vowel of first syllable 2. second radical 3. vowel of second syllable 4. third radical 5. first radical 6. root

1.2.3. 1. bá3at 2. ḥáḍar 3. wáṣal 4. dáras 5. 3ámal 6. ráʔaṣ 7. ṭálab 8. xárag 9. láḥam 10. náfa3

1.3.1. 1. kátabit 2. ṭálabit 3. 3ámalit 4. ḍárabit 5. náfa3it 6. fátaḥit

1.3.2. 1. she wrote 2. she requested 3. she worked 4. she hit 5. it was useful 6. she opened

1.3.3. 1. kátabu 2. ṭálabu 3. 3ámalu 4. ḍárabu 5. náfa3u 6. fátaḥu

1.3.4.

					n		ḥ	
			w	a	ṣ	a	f	u
				t		r		
		ḥ	ʃ	a	k	a	r	u
		a		?		?		
	b		s			i		u
d	a	f	a	3	i	t		
s		ḥ		b				
ḥ	a	r	a	s	i	t		
r		s		t				
ḥ	a	l	a	?				
			?					

1.3.5. 1. katábt you wrote 2. ṭalábt you requested 3. ḍarábt you hit 4. ʃakárt you thanked 5. xarágt you exited 6. waṣáft you described

1.3.6. 1. katábti 2. ṭalábti 3. ḍarábti 4. ʃakárti 5. xarágti 6. waṣáfti

1.3.7. 1. katábtu 2. ṭalábtu 3. ḍarábtu 4. ʃakártu 5. xarágtu 6. waṣáftu

1.3.8. 1. katábt, katábti, katábtu 2. xarágt, xarágti, xarágtu 3. ḥasábt, ḥasábti, ḥasábtu 4. darást, darásti, darástu 5. 3amált, 3amálti, 3amáltu

1.3.9. 1. gáma3 2. rásamit 3. ʔá3adu 4. ṭabáxt 5. wazánti 6. kasártu 7. ɣásalu 8. lámasit 9. rakánt 10. dáxal

1.3.10. 1. rasámt I drew 2. ṭalábt I requested 3. 3amált I did 4. katábt I wrote 5. wazánt I weighed 6. gamá3t I collected

1.3.11. 1. rasámna we drew 2. ṭalábna we requested 3. 3amálna we did 4. katábna we wrote 5. wazánna we weighed 6. gamá3na we collected

1.3.12. 1. náṭaʔt 2. ʔa3ádna 3. 3amált 4. lamásti 5. ṭalábtu 6. kásar 7. ɣásalit 8. ṭábaxu

1.3.13.

	explained	spent	swept
ána	ʃaráḥt	ṣaráft	kanást
íḥna	ʃaráḥna	ṣaráfna	kanásna
ínta	ʃaráḥt	ṣaráft	kanást
ínti	ʃaráḥti	ṣaráfti	kanásti
íntu	ʃaráḥtu	ṣaráftu	kanástu
húwwa	ʃáraḥ	ṣáraf	kánas
híyya	ʃáraḥit	ṣárafit	kánasit
húmma	ʃáraḥu	ṣárafu	kánasu

1.3.14. 1. eight 2. húwwa 3. híyya 4. húmma 5. remains on the first syllable 6. consonant 7. shift to the second syllable 8. ána 9. ínta

1.3.15. 1. he understood 2. he heard 3. I drank / you (m.) drank 4. we knew 5. he got dressed 6. you (pl.) caught 7. you (f.) lived 8. she played

1.3.16. 1. híyya (third-person feminine singular) and húmma (third-person plural) 2. i and u (Note: This does not occur for s1-3 verbs because *a* cannot elide.)

1.3.17. 1. she understood 2. she heard 3. they got dresed 4. they caught

1.3.18. 1. fihímt 2. sím3u 3. ʃírbit 4. 3irífti 5. ʃiríbtu 6. libísna 7. mískit 8. líbsu 9. 3írfit 10. fihímt

1.3.19. 1. díḥik 2. fíʃlit 3. ḥílmu 4. kibírt 5. lí3bu 6. rikíbti 7. 3íṭsu 8. nizílt 9. wíldit 10. sikítna

1.3.20. 1. darást 2. you (f.) caught 3. naṭaʔti 4. I drank / you (m.) drank 5. kásar 6. we heard 7. ḥálaʔit 8. you (pl.) studied 9. fíhmu 10. she did 11. dafá3t 12. he sneezed 13. ɣasálna 14. she got dressed 15. lamástu 16. you (pl.) sat 17. ḥílmit 18. they calculated 19. sáraʔu 20. he weighed

1.4.1. 1. makatábʃ he didn't write 2. maṭalábʃ he didn't request 3. maḍarábʃ he didn't hit 4. mafhímʃ he didn't remember 5. masmí3ʃ he didn't hear 6. malbísʃ he didn't get dressed

1.4.2. 1. makatabítʃ she didn't write 2. maṭalabítʃ she didn't request 3. maḍarabítʃ she didn't hit 4. mafhmítʃ she didn't remember 5. masim3ítʃ she didn't hear 6. malibsítʃ she didn't get dressed

1.4.3. 1. maṭalabúʃ they didn't write 2. maḍarabúʃ they didn't hit 3. masim3úʃ they didn't hear 4. mafihmúʃ they didn't understand

1.4.4. 1. madarástiʃ 2. ma3amáltiʃ 3. mafihímtiʃ 4. mafihímtiʃ

1.4.5. 1. marakántiʃ 2. madħiktiʃ 3. maʃʃiltúʃ 4. maʃaraħúʃ 5. makatabnāʃ 6. makasártiʃ 7. maʃribtíʃ 8. mafataħtúʃ 9. malabasúʃ 10. masaraʔnāʃ

1.4.6.

	didn't do	didn't play
ána	ma3amáltiʃ	mal3íbtiʃ
íħna	ma3amalnāʃ	mal3ibnāʃ
ínta	ma3amáltiʃ	mal3íbtiʃ
ínti	ma3amaltíʃ	mal3ibtíʃ
íntu	ma3amaltúʃ	mal3ibtúʃ
húwwa	ma3amálʃ	mal3íbʃ
híyya	ma3amalítʃ	mali3bítʃ
húmma	ma3amalúʃ	mali3búʃ

1.4.7. 1. a prefix and a suffix 2. lengthened 3. íħna, ínti, íntu, húmma 4. i 5. ána, ínta 6. two adjacent consonants (namely, ána and ínta)

1.4.8.

	negative perfect
ána	ma-___-tiʃ
íħna	ma-___-nāʃ
ínta	ma-___-tiʃ
ínti	ma-___-tíʃ
íntu	ma-___-túʃ
húwwa	ma-___-ʃ
híyya	m-___-ítʃ
húmma	ma-___-úʃ

1.4.9. 4. ʃiríbna 5. katábna 6. kátabu 7. makatabúʃ 8. makatabtúʃ 9. makatábtiʃ 10. malbístiʃ 11. malibsítʃ 12. malibsúʃ 13. líbsu 14. líbis 15. libíst 16. libíst 17. malbístiʃ 18. ma3amáltiʃ 19. ma3amalítʃ 20. mafihmítʃ

1.5.1. 1. yíḍrab 2. yíktib 3. yímsik 4. yúskun 5. yúṭlub 6. yíʃrab

1.5.2. 1. yíħḍar 2. yílmis 3. yúdxul 4. yífham 5. yílbis 6. yúskut

1.5.3. 1. removing 2. sometimes 3. 1s2, 1s3, 1s4, 1s6 4. 1s1, 1s5 5. prefix 6. i 7. u

1.5.4.

table	perfect húwwa form	imperfect húwwa form
1s1	CáCaC	yíCCaC
1s2	CáCaC	yíCCiC
1s3	CáCaC	yúCCuC
1s4	CíCiC	yíCCaC
1s5	CíCiC	yíCCiC
1s6	CíCiC	yúCCuC

1.5.5.

1s1	1s2	1s3	1s4	1s5
bá3at *send*	dáfa3 *pay*	ʔá3ad *sit*	díħik *laugh*	líbis *get dressed*
báħas *research*	dáras *study*	dáxal *enter*	fíhim *understand*	mísik *catch*
ḍárab *hit*	ɣásal *wash*	ħáras *guard*	fíʃil *fail*	nízil *descend*
fátaħ *open*	ħásab *calculate*	kánas *sweep*	ħílim *dream*	wílid *give birth*
gáma3 *gather*	kátab *write*	ráʔaṣ *dance*	kíbir *grow up*	
ħáḍar *attend*	láħam *heal*	ʃákar *thank*	lí3ib *play*	**1s6**
ħálaʔ *shave*	lámas *touch*	ṭábax *cook*	ríkib *ride*	síkin *live*
kásar *break*	rákan *park*	ṭálab *request*	sími3 *hear*	síkit *be quiet*
náfa3 *be useful*	rásam *draw*	xárag *exit*	ʃírib *drink*	
náṭaʔ *pronounce*	ʃáraf *spend*	3írif *know*		
sáraʔ *steal*	wáṣaf *describe*	3íṭis *sneeze*		
ʃáraħ *explain*	wázan *weigh*			
wáṣal *arrive*	3ámal *do, make*			

1.5.6. 1s1: yíb3at, yíbħas, yídfa3, yíḍrab, yíftaħ, yígma3, yíħḍar, yíħlaʔ, yíksar, yínfa3, yínṭaʔ, yísraʔ, yíʃraħ, yíwṣal; 1s2: yídris, yíɣsil, yíħsib, yíktib, yílħim, yílmis, yírkin, yírsim, yíṣrif, yíwṣif, yíwzin, yí3mil; 1s3: yúʔud, yúdxul, yúħrus, yúknus, yúrʔuṣ, yúʃkur, yúṭbux, yúṭlub, yúxrug; 1s4: yídħak, yífham, yíffal, yíħlam, yíkbar, yíl3ab, yírkab, yísma3, yíʃrab, yí3raf, yí3ṭas; 1s5: yílbis, yímsik, yínzil, yíwlid; 1s6: yúskun, yúskut

1.5.7. 1. He needs to study. 2. He wants to explain. 3. He needs to get dressed. 4. He wants to dance. 5. He needs to be quiet. 6. He wants to drink.

1.5.8. 1. 3áyza tíl3ab 2. lāzim tífham 3. 3áyza tísma3 4. 3áyza tíwlid 5. lāzim tí3raf 6. lāzim túxrug

1.5.9. 1. c. 2. a. 3. c. 4. b. 5. b. 6. c.

1.5.10. 1. We want to dance. 2. You (m.) want to get dressed. 3. She wants to laugh. 4. We need to be quiet. 5. He wants to drink. 6. She needs to study. / You (m.) need to study. 7. We want to drink. 8. He needs to research.

1.5.11. 1. 3āyiz yíħlam 2. lāzim tígma3 3. 3ayzīn nígma3 4. lāzim tíħlam 5. 3áyza tídris 6. 3āyiz tídris 7. lāzim núṭbux 8. lāzim yúṭbux

1.5.12. 1. I need to study. 2. I might cook. 3. I (m.) want to dance. 4. I might drink.

1.5.13. 1. musta3ídd áṭbux 2. musta3ídda áṭbux 3. nāwi tídris 4. náwya tídris 5. 3áyza áʃrab 6. lāzim ábħas 7. nawyīn níʃrab 8. nāwi áskut

1.5.14.

	positive imperfect
ána	á-___
íħna	ní-___ / nú-___
ínta	tí-___ / tú-___
ínti	ti-___-i / tu-___-i
íntu	ti-___-u / tu-___-u
húwwa	yí-___ / yú-___
híyya	tí-___ / tú-___
húmma	yi-___-u / yu-___-u

1.5.15. 1. You (f.) need to study. 2. We want to explain. 3. You (pl.) are willing to get dressed. 4. She wants to dance. 5. You (f.) want to dance. 6. They intend to drink.

1.5.16. 1. lāzim tídris 2. lāzim níʃraħ 3. 3ayzīn tilbísu 4. lāzim túrʔuṣ 5. náwya turʔúṣi 6. nāwi/náwya áʃrab

1.5.17. Numbers 1, 4, 5, and 9 are incorrect.

1.5.18.

	fíhim	fátaħ	dáxal
ána	áfham	áftaħ	ádxul
íħna	nífham	níftaħ	núdxul
ínta	tífham	tíftaħ	túdxul
ínti	tifhámi	tiftáħi	tudxúli
íntu	tifhámu	tiftáħu	tudxúlu
húwwa	yífham	yíftaħ	yúdxul
híyya	tífham	tíftaħ	túdxul
húmma	yifhámu	yiftáħu	yudxúlu

1.6.1.

	positive	negative
ána	áksar	maksárʃ
íħna	níksar	maniksárʃ
ínta	tíksar	matiksárʃ
ínti	tiksári	matiksarīʃ
íntu	tiksáru	matiksarūʃ
húwwa	yíksar	mayiksárʃ
híyya	tíksar	matiksárʃ
húmma	yiksáru	mayiksarūʃ

1.6.2.

	incorrect	corrected
ána	maawṣáfʃ	mawṣáfʃ
íħna	maníwṣafʃ	maniwṣáfʃ
ínta	matiwṣáfʃ	(correct)
ínti	matiwṣafíʃ	matiwṣafīʃ
íntu	matiwṣáfūʃ	matiwṣafūʃ
húwwa	mawaṣáfʃ	mayiwṣáfʃ
híyya	mayiwṣáfʃ	matiwṣáfʃ
húmma	mayiṣafūʃ	mayiwṣafūʃ

1.6.3. 1. mayib3átʃ 2. manidrísʃ 3. matuxrúgʃ 4. maʃʃálʃ 5. matilbisīʃ 6. mayuskutūʃ 7. mayiʃrabūʃ 8. matisraʔūʃ 9. matuknusūʃ 10. maħsíbʃ 11. matilmísʃ 12. matisma3ūʃ 13. manikbárʃ 14. matirkinīʃ 15. maʃrábʃ 16. matuʃkurūʃ 17. mayigma3ūʃ 18. matiṣrifīʃ 19. maniħḍárʃ 20. matidħákʃ

1.6.4. 1. I need to (have to/must) study 2. we mustn't hit 3. you (f.) don't have to (don't need to) drink 4. you (m.) don't need to (don't have to) understand / she doesn't need to (doesn't have to) understand 5. they mustn't cook 6. he mustn't write

1.6.5. 1. miʃ lāzim tidrísi 2. lāzim matiḍrábʃ 3. lāzim matiʃrabūʃ 4. miʃ lāzim nil3áb 5. lāzim tífham 6. lāzim mayuʔ3údʃ

1.7.1.

1s1 ḍárab		1s2 kátab		1s3 ṭálab	
tíḍrab	íḍrab	tíktib	íktib	tútlub	útlub
tiḍrábi	iḍrábi	tiktíbi	iktíbi	tutlúbi	utlúbi
tiḍrábu	iḍrábu	tiktíbu	iktíbu	tutlúbu	utlúbu

1. The initial t- is dropped.

1.7.2. 1. i3mil, i3míli, i3mílu 2. ídris, idrísi, idrísu 3. íʃraħ, iʃráħi, iʃráħu 4. úskut, uskúti, uskútu 5. úʔ3ud, uʔ3údi, uʔ3údu 6. ísma3, ismá3i, ismá3u

1.7.3. 1. They are not different; they are identical.

1.7.4. 1. matisráʔʃ, matisraʔīʃ, matisraʔūʃ 2. matidfá3ʃ, matidfa3īʃ, matidfa3ūʃ 3. matudxúlʃ, matudxulīʃ, matudxulūʃ 4. matidħákʃ, matidħakīʃ, matidħakūʃ 5. matuʔ3údʃ, matuʔ3udīʃ, matuʔ3udūʃ

1.7.5. 1. iʃrábi 2. matiʃrabūʃ 3. matiʃrábʃ 4. mati3mílʃ 5. i3mil 6. i3mílu 7. i3míli 8. uxrúgi 9. matuxrugīʃ 10. matuxrúgʃ 11. matidrísʃ 12. matidrisīʃ 13. matidrisūʃ 14. idrísu 15. irkábu 16. matirkabūʃ 17. matirkabīʃ 18. matirkábʃ 19. írkab 20. íʃrab

1.8.1. 1. ħa- 2. the imperfect tense 3. It is assimilated. 4. by adding miʃ before the verb

1.8.2. 1. I will dance 2. we won't explain 3. you (m.) will ride / she will ride 4. you (f.) will study 5. you (pl.) will get dressed 6. he won't do 7. she will park / you (m.) will park 8. they won't drink

1.8.3. 1. miʃ ħatúxrug 2. ħanídfa3 3. ħatuskútu 4. miʃ ħatísma3 5. ħál3ab 6. miʃ ħayifʃálu

1.9.1. 1. The bi- imperfect is formed by adding bi- to the bare imperfect forms. 2. Yes. It is assimilated before the a- of the first personal singular (ána) form. 3. No. The vowel is always i, regardless of the vowel in the personal prefix.

1.9.2. 1. biyíḍrab 2. bitífham 3. binúdxul 4. bámsik 5. biyiktíbu 6. biyíʃrab

1.9.3.

	ʃírib	kátab	ṭálab
ána	báʃrab	báktib	báṭlub
íḥna	biníʃrab	biníktib	binúṭlub
ínta	bitíʃrab	bitíktib	bitúṭlub
ínti	bitiʃrábi	bitiktíbi	bituṭlúbi
íntu	bitiʃrábu	bitiktíbu	bituṭlúbu
húwwa	biyíʃrab	biyíktib	biyúṭlub
híyya	bitíʃrab	bitíktib	bitúṭlub
húmma	biyiʃrábu	biyiktíbu	biyuṭlúbu

1.9.4. 1. he hits 2. you (m.) understand / she understands 3. we enter 4. I catch 5. they write

1.9.5. 1. we're doing 2. I'm studying 3. you (f.) are parking 4. he's riding 5. they're writing

1.9.6.

dáras (study)
ána bádris
íḥna bnídris
ínta btídris
ínti btidrísi
íntu btidrísu
húwwa byídris
híyya btídris
húmma byidrísu

1.9.7. 1. karīm biyí3mil wi nágwa btí3mil kamān. 2. sāmi byíl3ab wi sāmiḥ biyíl3ab kamān. 3. zēnab bitíbḥas wi 3azīza btíbḥas kamān. 4. 3abīr bitíɣsil wi hāni byíɣsil kamān. 5. múṣṭafa byílbas wi fáṭma btílbas kamān.

1.10.1. 1. mabyuṭbúxʃ he doesn't cook 2. mabtiʃrábʃ you (m.) don't drink / she doesn't drink 3. mabyi3rafúʃ they don't know 4. mabni3mílʃ we don't do 5. mabtidfa3íʃ you (f.) don't pay 6. mabtidḥakúʃ you (pl.) don't laugh 7. mabarsímʃ I don't know 8. mabyiftáḥʃ he doesn't open 9. mabtisráʔʃ you (m.) don't steal / she doesn't steal 10. mabtuḥrúsʃ you (m.) don't guard / she doesn't guard

1.10.2. 1. mabaskútʃ 2. mabalbísʃ 3. mabasmá3ʃ 4. mabaɣsílʃ 5. mabaʃkúrʃ 6. mabaḥláʔʃ

1.10.3. 1. mabniwṣífʃ 2. mabniɣsílʃ 3. mabnismá3ʃ 4. mabnuskúnʃ 5. mabnuʃkúrʃ 6. mabniḥláʔʃ

1.10.4. 1. mabtuskúnʃ 2. mabtigmá3ʃ 3. mabtiwṣíſf 4. mabtiɣsílʃ 5. mabtinṭáʔʃ 6. mabtiḥláʔʃ

1.10.5. 1. mabtigma3íʃ 2. mabtiwṣafíʃ 3. mabtuskuníʃ 4. mabtiḥlámíʃ 5. mabtuknusíʃ 6. mabtinṭaʔíʃ

1.10.6. 1. mabtiḥlámúʃ 2. mabtuknusúʃ 3. mabtiktibúʃ 4. mabtigma3úʃ 5. mabtilḥimúʃ 6. mabtinṭaʔúʃ

1.10.7. 1. mabyiḥlámʃ 2. mabyuknúsʃ 3. mabyiʃfálʃ 4. mabyiftáḥʃ 5. mabyiktíbʃ 6. mabyilḥímʃ

1.10.8. 1. mabtiwlídʃ 2. mabtiʃfálʃ 3. mabtilḥímʃ 4. mabtiftáḥʃ 5. mabtiktíbʃ 6. mabtirkábʃ

1.10.9. 1. mabyiftaḥúʃ 2. mabyidrisúʃ 3. mabyiwlidúʃ 4. mabyirkabúʃ 5. mabyiksarúʃ 6. mabyiʃfalúʃ

1.10.10. 1. mabaʃrábʃ 2. yūsif mabyi3ráſf 3. márwa mabti3mílʃ 4. mabti3rafúʃ 5. mabniftáḥʃ 6. yásmin wi farīda mabyidḥakúʃ 7. mabasrá3ʃ 8. mabtidfa3íʃ 9. mabyi3ráſf 10. mabtuḥrúsʃ

1.11.1. 1. identical 2. ā 3. i 4. -a 5. elide 6. shorten 7. -īn 8. the same 9. final

1.11.2. 1. doing 2. studying 3. writing 4. knowing 5. living 6. wearing

1.11.3. 1. fātiḥ 2. ɣāsil 3. rākib 4. ʔā3id 5. fāhim 6. xārig

1.11.4. 1. fátḥa 2. ɣásla 3. rákba 4. ʔá3da 5. fáhma 6. xárga

1.11.5. 1. ḥadrīn 2. nazlīn 3. ṭalbīn 4. daxlīn 5. la3bīn 6. ʔa3dīn

1.11.6. 1. íḥna faʃlīn. 2. ínta kānis. 3. húwwa líssa ḥāliʔ. 4. fáṭma miʃ dáf3a. 5. ána fátḥa. 6. húmma líssa ʃarḥīn. 7. ána líssa 3āmil. 8. ínti miʃ kánsa 9. íntu líssa fatḥīn 10. karīm miʃ ḥāliʔ.

1.12.1.

	ʃírib	kásar	wílid
masc.	maʃrūb	maksūr	mawlūd
fem.	maʃrūba	maksūra	mawlūda
plural	maʃrubīn	maksurīn	mawludīn

1.12.2.

```
n m m r ʃ w m a ū m m x l m s x ẓ
m m a d r ū s a m a a ḍ m a r l i
z i w k i ṭ a m k a f ħ ū k n z m
m a l ū t a m t ā ʃ h a r s ū n a
a a u ū ḍ u ū a ṭ ā ū k i u k ā w
ħ ʃ d g ā b s a r n m r b n s y z
r r ī f b a r m ū s a a a i a ī u
u ş n ħ ū m a k s r ī n f n m b n
s i k i n 3 m i m a ɣ s u l ī n ī
i ṭ m a r r ū g m a d r u s n a n
m a w ū z i n w a ş ā ɣ m a m r l
m a f h u m a ɣ s u l a ʃ ẓ x m f
k a t a b f u r 3 a m a f h m ī n
```

masculine	feminine	plural
maktūb	madrūsa	mawludīn
madfū3	mafhūma	maħrusīn
marsūm	maksūra	mawzunīn
maskūn	ma3rūfa	maɣsulīn

1.13.1. *Only the corrected forms are shown below.*

	positive	negative	
ána		marakántiʃ	**perfect**
íħna	sikínna		
ínta	lamást		
ínti		mafhimtíʃ	
íntu	katábtu		
húwwa	ʃirib	maħlímʃ	
híyya	nízlit		
húmma		maħasabúʃ	

ána		manfá3ʃ	**imperfect**
íħna	níħras		
ínta			
ínti	tidħáki		
íntu	tudxúlu	matirkabúʃ	
húwwa	yíkbar	mayib3átʃ	
híyya			
húmma		mayilħimūʃ	

ána			**bi-imperfect**
íħna	biníl3ab	mabniysílʃ	
ínta		mabtu?3údiʃ	
ínti	bituskúti	mabtuṭbuxīʃ	
íntu			
húwwa	biyíwzin	mabyi3mílʃ	
híyya			
húmma			

ána	ħársim	miʃ ħársim	**future**
íħna	ħaníħla?	miʃ ħaníħla?	
ínta	ħatí3ṭas		
ínti	ħatinṭá?i		
íntu			
húwwa			
híyya		miʃ ħatíwlid	
húmma			

ínta	íktib		**imperative**
ínti	udxúli	matudxulíʃ	
íntu			

	active	passive	
masculine		maktūb	**participles**
feminine	kátba		
plural		mawludīn	

1.13.2.

	writing	cooking	drinking
3áli	X		X
máryam		X	X
áħmad	X	X	
múna	X	X	

1. máryam bitíktib. 2. 3áli <u>byúṭbux</u>. 3. áħmad wi múna <u>byiʃrábu</u>. / múna w- áħmad biyiʃrábu.

1.13.3. 1. bá3atit 2. ħayídris 3. sákna 4. 3ayzīn yil3ábu 5. biyísra? 6. miʃ ħaníbħas 7. malamástiʃ 8. mati3mílʃ 9. maktūb 10. lāzim ti3ráfu 11. 3áyiz áʃkur 12. húmma líssa ṭabxīn 13. mabtiftáħʃ 14. xarágna 15. matiktibīʃ 16. bayínfa3 17. ur?úṣu 18. 3áli byi3ṭas 19. maħaḍartíʃ 20. ríkbit

2.1.1.

1h1	ʃāf see	ṭār fly
?āl say	zār visit	3āʃ live
bās kiss	3ām swim	**1h3**
fāt pass	**1h2**	bāt stay overnight
kān be	bā3 sell	nām sleep
māt die	gāb bring	**1h4**
rāħ go	sāb leave	xāf be afraid, worry

2.1.2. 1. he went 2. she kissed 3. they brought 4. she flew 5. they swam 6. he didn't go 7. she didn't kiss 8. they didn't bring 9. he didn't fly 10. he didn't swim

2.1.3. 1. ʃāf 2. zāru 3. ?ālit 4. nāmit 5. bā3u 6. maʃáfʃ 7. mazarūʃ 8. ma?alítʃ 9. manamítʃ 10. maba3úʃ

2.1.4. 1. we saw 2. you (pl.) saw 3. I said / you (m.) said 4. you (f.) slept 5. I sold / you (m.) sold 6. we weren't afraid 7. I didn't go / you (m.) didn't go 8. you (pl.) didn't bring 9. you (f.) didn't fly 10. we didn't swim

2.1.5.

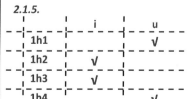

	i	u
1h1		√
1h2	√	
1h3	√	
1h4		√

1. sibt 2. 3íʃna 3. kúnti 4. bitt 5. māt 6. mabústiʃ 7. fúttu 8. maruħtūʃ 9. nimt 10. magabūʃ

2.1.6. 1. I want to sleep 2. we visit / we're visiting 3. I bring / I'm bringing 4. I'll go 5. you (f.) musn't sell 6. she doesn't want to say 7. they leave / they're leaving 8. he isn't afraid 9. you (m.) don't want to say

2.1.7. 1. 1h3 and 1h4 2. 1h2 3. 1h1

2.1.8. 1. maniɡíbʃ 2. mabinizúrʃ 3. biyiʔūl 4. mabiyiʔulūʃ 5. mabitinamūʃ 6. bitirūḥ 7. nūra bitirūḥ 8. mabitirúḥʃ 9. nūra mabitirúḥʃ

2.1.9. 1. c 2. b 3. b 4. d 5. b

2.1.10.

	positive	negative
ínta	rāḥ	matrúḥʃ
ínti	rāḥi	matruḥīʃ
íntu	rāḥu	matruḥūʃ

1. Go! 2. Don't go!

2.1.11. 1. 3ām, 3āmi, 3āmu 2. matnámʃ, matnamīʃ, matnamūʃ 3. ɡīb / hāt, ɡībi / hāti, ɡību / hātu 4. matkúnʃ, matkunīʃ, matkunūʃ 5. xāf, xāfi, xāfu 6. matbi3ʃ, matbi3īʃ, matbi3ūʃ

2.1.12.

	active	passive
masculine	bāyi3	mitbā3
feminine	báy3a	mitbā3a
plural	bay3īn	mitba3īn

2.1.13. 1. kān 2. bāsu 3. ḥay3ūmu 4. mabitnámʃ 5. 3áyza tṭīr 6. mamátʃ 7. mabtizrīʃ 8. lāzim nibī3 9. biybātu 10. múna bti3īʃ

2.1.14. 1. Sāmi is going 2. he goes 3. she's going 4. Rīm goes 5. you (pl.) are going 6. they go 7. I (m.) am not going 8. I don't go 9. Rīm isn't going 10. they're going 11. you (f.) are going 12. they don't go

2.2.1.
1d1 ʔára read, báʔa become, ɡára happen, mála fill; **1d2** báda begin, báka cry, bána build, 3áfa forgive, ráma throw; **1d3** rāɡa implore; **1d4** díri realize, ṣíḥi wake up, nísi forget, hídi calm down; **1d5** ɡíri run, míʃi walk

2.2.2. 1. málit 2. rámu 3. rāɡit 4. málu 5. bádit 6. bánu 7. báka 8. 3áfu 9. báʔit 10. ɡárit

2.2.3. 1. díryit 2. nísyu 3. ṣíḥyit 4. míʃyu 5. ɡíri 6. ɡíryu

2.2.4. 1. she was quiet 2. they read 3. they didn't read 4. he didn't fill 5. she became 6. they didn't become 7. he wasn't quiet 8. she didn't forget 9. they didn't forget 10. they didn't throw

2.2.5. 1. malēt 2. ramēt 3. nisīna 4. ɡirīti 5. ṣiḥīt 6. miʃītu 7. 3afētu 8. bakēt 9. hidīna 10. banēti

2.2.6. 1. maramítʃ I didn't throw / you (m.) didn't throw 2. mamalináʃ we didn't fill 3. maraɡitīʃ you (f.) didn't implore 4. manisīʃ he didn't forget 5. maʔaritūʃ you (pl.) didn't read 6. mamíʃyítʃ she didn't walk 7. maɡiryūʃ they didn't run 8. mabadināʃ we didn't begin 9. maṣiḥīʃ he didn't get up

2.2.7. 1. mamalítʃ 2. maramítʃ 3. mansināʃ 4. maɡritīʃ 5. maʃḥítʃ 6. mamʃitūʃ 7. ma3aftūʃ 8. mabakítʃ 9. mahdināʃ 10. mabantīʃ

2.2.8. 1. ʔarēt 2. maʔarítʃ 3. ʔarēt 4. maʔarnāʃ 5. ɡíryit 6. maɡiryūʃ 7. díri 8. madritūʃ 9. bakēti 10. mabakítʃ

2.2.9. 2. mabaʔátʃ 3. mabaʔátʃ 4. baʔēt 5. nisīt 6. nísyu 7. manisyūʃ 8. mabadūʃ 9. mabadítʃ 10. mabadtīʃ 11. badēti 12. nisīna 13. mansināʃ 14. maramnāʃ 15. maramāʃ 16. mamʃīʃ 17. míʃi 18. miʃītu 19. míʃyit 20. mamíʃyítʃ

2.2.10. 1. I want to walk 2. we forget 3. I implore / I'm imploring 4. I'll throw 5. you (f.) musn't fill 6. she doesn't want to be quiet 7. they build / they're building 8. he doesn't forgive 9. you (m.) don't want to read

2.2.11. 1. 1d2 2. a and a 3. i 4. a 5. ráɡa 6. u 7. a 8. i and i 9. changes from that of

2.2.12 1. I begin / I'm beginning 2. you (m.) want to run 3. you (f.) want to run / she wants to run 4. he will cry 5. you (m./f.) run / you're running / she runs / she's running 6. he won't forgive

2.2.13. 1. I don't read / I'm not reading 2. he needs to forget 3. you (m.) calm down / are calming down / she calms down / is calming down 4. he doesn't realize 5. we mustn't fill 6. it won't happen

2.2.14. 1. iṣḥa, iṣḥi, iṣḥu 2. ma3tiʔrāʃ, ma3tiʔrīʃ, ma3tiʔrūʃ 3. íɡri, íɡri, íɡru 4. matibkīʃ, matibkīʃ, matibkūʃ

2.2.15.

	ʔára	bána	díri	
masc.	ʔāri	bāni	dāri	active
fem.	ʔárya	bánya	dárya	
plural	ʔaryīn	banyīn	daryīn	
masc.	máʔri	mábni	mádri	passive
fem.	maʔríyya	mabníyya	madríyya	
plural	maʔriyīn	mabniyīn	madriyīn	

2.2.16. 1. mamʃīʃ 2. mamíʃyítʃ 3. mamiʃyūʃ 4. mabanūʃ 5. mabyibnūʃ 6. mabtibnīʃ 7. bitíbni 8. bitínsa 9. mabtinsāʃ 10. matinsāʃ 11. ínsa 12. ḥatínsa 13. ḥanínsa 14. ḥaniʔra 15. íḥna ʔaryīn 16. híyya ʔárya 17. lāzim tíʔra 18. maʔríyya 19. miʃ maʔríyya 20. maʔarítʃ

2.3.1. 1. it was appropriate 2. he looked 3. she put 4. they answered 5. she entered 6. they thought 7. I loved / you (m.) loved 8. you (f.) felt 9. we became bored 10. you (pl.) counted

2.3.2. 1. ṣáḥḥu 2. baṣṣēt 3. ḥattēt 4. raddēna 5. xaʃʃēti 6. ẓánnit 7. ḥabbētu 8. ḥass 9. mallēt 10. 3áddit

2.3.3. 1. maṣáḥḥiʃ 2. mabaṣṣitʃ 3. maḥabbítʃ 4. mamallítʃ 5. maẓannināʃ 6. maxáʃʃiʃ 7. maradditíʃ 8. ma3addūʃ 9. maḥassítʃ 10. maḥáṭṭiʃ

2.3.4. 1. it needs to be appropriate 2. she intends to answer 3. he wants to count 4. we are willing to enter 5. I need to love 6. they want to think 7. I (f.) don't want to look (The imperfect form is abúṣṣ, but the a- assimilates when preceded by a vowel.) 8. we don't want to become bored. 9. you (m.) don't need to put 10. you (pl.) are willing to feel

2.3.5. 1. so that you (f.) love 2. so that I put 3. so that they count 4. so that I don't look 5. because I don't look 6. so that they think 7. so that we don't become bored 8. because you (m.) answer / because she answers 9. because it's appropriate 10. because you (pl.) don't enter

2.3.6. 1. c 2. c 3. a 4. c 5. b 6. c

2.3.7. 1. baḥíbb 2. bit3ídd 3. binxúʃʃ 4. bitrúddi 5. biyẓúnnu 6. bitḥúṭṭu 7. biyḥíss 8. bitmíll 9. binṣáḥḥ 10. bitbúṣṣ

2.3.8. 1. mabaḥíbbiʃ 2. mabit3íddiʃ 3. mabinxúʃʃiʃ 4. mabitruddíʃ 5. mabiyẓunnūʃ 6. mabitḥuṭṭūʃ 7. mabiyḥíssiʃ 8. mabitmílliʃ 9. mabinṣáḥḥiʃ 10. mabitbúṣṣiʃ

2.3.9. 1. miʃ ḥaẓúnn 2. ḥat3ídd 3. ḥanbúṣṣ 4. ḥatḥíss 5. miʃ ḥayṣáḥḥu 6. ḥatxúʃʃi 7. miʃ ḥayḥíbb 8. ḥatmíllu 9. ḥaxúʃʃ 10. miʃ ḥaybúṣṣ

2.3.10. 1. ʔuṣṣ, ʔúṣṣi, ʔúṣṣu 2. mat3úḍḍiʃ, mat3uḍḍíʃ, mat3uḍḍūʃ 3. ḥill, ḥílli, ḥíllu 4. matɣíʃʃiʃ, matɣiʃʃíʃ, matɣiʃʃūʃ

2.3.11.

	ʃakk	sabb	
masc.	ʃākik	sābib	active
fem.	ʃákka	sábba	
plural	ʃakkīn	sabbīn	
masc.	maʃkūk	masbūb	passive
fem.	maʃkūka	masbūba	
plural	maʃkukīn	masbubīn	

2.3.12. 1. mabitṣáḥḥiʃ 2. bitḥíbbi 3. ḥaṭṭēna 4. baʃúkk / bitʃúkk 5. raddēt / ráddit 6. maḥássiʃ 7. mabiy3iddūʃ 8. bitṣúmmu

2.4.1. 1. ʔult 2. baẓúnn 3. bádya 4. xáʃʃu 5. maḥássiʃ 6. íḥda 7. mabtirmíʃ 8. bitzúru 9. fāyit 10. lāzim manʃúfiʃ

2.4.2.

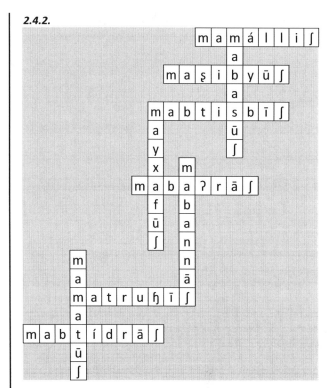

3.1. 1. kátabit 2. ríkbit 3. ríkbu 4. bā3u 5. bi3t 6. mabí3tiʃ 7. mabí3tiʃ 8. mabi3tíʃ 9. maʔultíʃ 10. mabitʔulíʃ 11. bitʔuli 12. binʔūl 13. binxāf 14. mabinxáffʃ 15. miʃ ḥanxāf 16. miʃ ḥaníʔra 17. lāzim maníʔrāʃ / miʃ lāzim níʔra 18. lāzim níʔra 19. lāzim yíʔra 20. 3áyiz yíʔra 21. 3áyza tíʔra 22. 3áyza tíʔri 23. ʔaréti 24. maʔartíʃ 25. mansitíʃ 26. mansitūʃ 27. manisyūʃ 28. nísyu 29. biyínsu 30. biy3íddu 31. biy3ídd 32.3idd 33. íʃraḥ 34. matiʃráḥʃ 35. ʃaráḥt 36. darást 37. ʃāriḥ 38. ʃarḥīn 39. baṣṣīn 40. bāṣiṣ 41. ḥabúṣṣ 42. ḥatbúṣṣ 43. ḥatbúṣṣ 44. baṣṣēt 45. baṣṣēt 46. báṣṣit 47. síknit 48. sikínt 49. katábt 50. kátab

3.2. 1. bábḥas 2. sáraʔit 3. binúʃkur 4. ḥayrūḥ 5. bakēt 6. mabaktíʃ 7. zurt 8. 3áyza -nām 9. miʃ ḥayḥíbbu 10. maḥattítʃ 11. ḥílmit 12. ráʔaʃit 13. nawyīn tidfá3u 14. mabyigríʃ 15. mabitgibūʃ 16. mabtuknúsʃ 17. rūḥ 18. il3ábi

4.1.1. 1. dárris 2. ʃáxxar 3. ʃáxxar 4. ʔánqaz 5. itgáwwiz 6. itfárrag 7. itgāwib 8. ityásal 9. infátaḥ 10. ixtálaf 11. iswádd 12. istáḥmil 13. istáɣrab 14. istiʔákkid 15. istiláʔʔaf 16. istibārik 17. ʃánkil 18. dáḥrag

4.1.2. 1. 5s1 2. 10s2 3. 4s 4. 9s 5. 3s 6. 6s 7. 7s2 8. 10.2s1

4.1.3. 1. 2d 2. 6d 3. 8g 4. 8h 5. 3d 6. 7h1 7. 10d 8. 4g

4.2.1. 1. gáḥḥiz he prepared 2. kammílit she completed 3. mawwítna we killed 4. masabbitūʃ they didn't stabilize 5. sallíft I lent 6. masallímtiʃ you (m.) didn't greet 7. ṣammímti you (f.) insisted 8. baxámmin I guess 9. ḥay3állim he will teach 10. bitdárrab she coaches 11. matdaxxánʃ (m.) don't smoke! 12. mabiyḥarrákʃ he doesn't move 13. miʃ ḥatnáḍḍaf you (m.)

won't clean 14. miqarrarīn (pl.) deciding 15. mabasárraḥ I'm not brushing 16. maṣaḥḥáḥtiʃ I didn't correct 17. miʃ ḥaywáʔʔaf he won't stop 18. bitxaṭṭáṭtu you (pl.) are planning 19. fakkártu you (pl.) thought 20. ɣannu (pl.) sing! 21. máḍḍu they spent 22. masammítʃ she didn't name 23. binṣalli we pray 24. warri (m.) show!

4.2.2. 1. biyfákkar 2. bitkámmil 3. 3allímt 4. wárra 5. ɣannētu 6. biymáḍḍi 7. basállif / bitsállif 8. bindárrab

4.2.3. 1. he thinks / he's thinking 2. she completes / she's completing 3. I taught 4. he showed 5. you (pl.) sang 6. he spends / he's spending (time) 7. I lend / I'm lending / you lend / you're lending 8. we coach / we're coaching

4.2.4. 1. maxamminʃ 2. masammāʃ 3. maba3allímʃ 4. mabiyṣammímʃ 5. magahhiznāʃ 6. mamawwíttiʃ 7. mabtiqarrarūʃ 8. mabiyḥarrakūʃ

4.2.5. 1. daxxánt 2. biysábbit 3. ḥanṣalli 4.3áyza -wárri 5. nāwi yiwáʔʔaf 6. mawwíttu 7. dárrabit 8. miʃ ḥaxámmin 9. mabiy3allímʃ 10. bitkámmil 11. sallímti 12. masarráḥʃ 13. lāzim niqárrar 14. lāzim mandaxxánʃ 15. biyxáṭṭaṭ 16. bitṣámmim 17. maṣaḥḥaḥtīʃ 18. bitɣanni 19. mabiyḥarrakūʃ 20. mabanáḍḍaf

4.2.6. 1. 3állim, 3allími, 3allímu 2. manaḍḍáfʃ, manaḍḍafīʃ, manaḍḍafūʃ 3. ṣálli, ṣálli, ṣállu 4. mawarrīʃ, mawarrīʃ, mawarrūʃ

4.2.7.

	gáhhiz	qárrar	wárra
masc.	migáhhiz	miqárrar	miwárri
fem.	migahhíza	miqarrára	miwarríyya
plural	migahhizīn	miqarrarīn	miwarriyīn

4.3.1. 1. meet 2. surprise 3. answer 4. try 5. help 6. travel 7. study 8. cure (treat) 9. avoid 10. call

4.3.2. 1. they met 2. she answered 3. I tried / you (m.) tried 4. we traveled 5. she studied 6. they cured 7. you (pl.) avoided 8. we called

4.3.3. 1. ʔáblu 2. dāwa 3. zakírti 4. nadēt / nādit 5. ḥawíltu 6. ʔabílt

4.3.4. 1. I (m.) want to help 2. we need to answer 3. I help / I'm helping 4. we answer / we're answering 5. he mustn't travel 6. he doesn't travel / he isn't traveling 7. he'll travel 8. he cures / he's curing 9. he doesn't cure / he isn't curing 10. you (pl.) avoid / you're avoiding 11. you (m./f.) avoid / you're avoiding / she avoids / she's avoiding 12. you (m.) help / you're helping / she helps / she's helping 13. you (m.) don't help / you're not helping / she doesn't help / she isn't helping 14. you (f.) help / you're helping 15. you (f.) don't help / you aren't helping 16. he'll try 17. he doesn't travel / he isn't traveling 18. you (f.) want to meet / she wants to meet 19. you (m.) want to meet 20. you (f.) mustn't

4.3.5. 1. maʔabíltiʃ 2. mabaʔabílʃ 3. sá3dit 4. sā3id 5. bitgáwbi 6. lāzim tigáwbi 7. lāzim tigāwib 8. ḥayḥáwlu 9. ḥayzákru 10. mabiyzakrūʃ

4.3.6. 1. dāwi 2. zákri 3. sá3du 4. ḥāwil 5. matfadíʃ 6. matfadīʃ 7. matsafrūʃ 8. sáfru 9. matnadūʃ 10. gáwbi

4.3.7. 1. I (m.) just studied 2. we just met 3. she just called 4. húmma líssa mdawyīn 5. ínta líssa msā3id 6. ána líssa mzákra

4.4.1.

table	perfect húwwa form	imperfect húwwa form
4s	ʔáCCaC	yíCCiC
4h	ʔaCāC	yiCīC
4d	ʔáCCa	yíCCi
4g	ʔaCáCC	yiCíCC

4.4.2. 1. she proved 2. they announced 3. you (f.) permitted 4. she canceled 5. we finished 6. I prepared / you (m.) prepared

4.4.3. 1. he didn't finish 2. I announced / you (m.) announced 3. he announces / he's announcing 4. he doesn't announce / he isn't announcing 5. you (m.) need to prepare / she needs to prepare 6. you (f.) need to prepare 7. they didn't cancel 8. we prove / we're proving 9. you (m./f.) will finish / she'll finish 10. they mustn't announce

4.4.4. 1. ʔa3lánt 2. maʔa3lántiʃ 3. maʔa3lántiʃ 4. mabti3línʃ 5. mabtinhīʃ 6. mabtinhīʃ 7. mabtinhūʃ 8. bitínhu 9. ḥatínhu 10. ḥánhi 11. ḥatīḥ 12. batīḥ 13. mabatíḥʃ 14. maʔatáḥtiʃ 15. maʔa3addítʃ 16. ʔa3addēt 17. ʔa3íddit 18. bit3ídd 19. bitísbit 20. biyisbítu

4.4.5. 1. i3lín 2. i3líni 3. ínhi 4. ínhu 5. mati3línʃ 6. matinhīʃ 7. itīḥu 8. mattiḥūʃ 9. íɣli 10. mat3iddīʃ

4.4.6. 1. ána líssa mu3lína 2. amīna líssa muɣlíyya 3. sa3īd líssa mtīḥ 4. íḥna líssa m3iddīn 5. ínta líssa múnhi 6. íntu líssa musbitīn

4.4.7. 1. mú3lan 2. mutāḥa 3. munhayīn 4. mu3ádd 5. múɣla 6. muɣlā (Notice that the feminine form is based on the masculine form +a, and since the defective masculine passive participle already ends in a, a + a assimilates into ā.)

4.4.8. 1. ʔú3lin 2. ʔuzhírit 3. ʔusīr 4. ʔúlqi 5. ʔuṣírr 6. ʔúlɣu (Notice that the final u is the third person plural suffix and does not vary form active to passive verbs, as is the case for all personal suffixes.)

4.4.9. 1. it was announced 2. it was shown 3. he was agitated 4. it was recited 5. it was insisted (on) 6. they were canceled

4.4.10. 1. it wasn't announced 2. it wasn't canceled 3. it is (being) proven 4. it is (being) canceled 5. it needs to be permitted 6. lāzim maytáḥʃ 7. ḥatúlɣa 8. biy3ádd 9. mabiyu3áddiʃ 10. maʔungízʃ

4.4.11.

```
ʔ  á  g  h  a  d  u  w  t  ī  ħ  x  m  u  3  ī  m
w  a  n  a  m  3  i  ṭ  ṣ  ṭ  ʃ  m  a  b  ī  ħ  a
a  ħ  g  u  u  l  ʔ  ú  3  d  i  m  ʔ  n  ʃ  a  b
r  ɣ  ā  ħ  s  u  ī  ʔ  ā  í  ẓ  b  u  a  f  t  y
t  a  m  ʔ  á  ī  f  h  ʃ  á  m  g  l  t  ā  i  i
b  ī  a  r  r  d  3  m  a  ʔ  u  l  ɣ  ī  ʃ  n  s
u  s  ʔ  a  r  í  i  l  m  h  s  l  ā  ʃ  s  q  b
ʔ  i  m  u  d  ɣ  a  t  u  a  ā  l  ʃ  t  b  í  í
n  m  a  ʔ  a  n  h  í  t  ʃ  r  ʔ  x  ī  a  z  t
m  ā  h  ū  z  s  ī  n  ʔ  u  ḍ  i  u  f  3  u  ʃ
a  n  ē  t  ʃ  ú  m  a  3  d  á  m  t  u  d  ī  ú
m  a  t  i  n  q  í  z  t  u  l  ɣ  á  ī  a  á  ʔ
u  ʔ  ʃ  t  h  á  x  ʔ  a  3  á  d  d  t  ħ  m  z
```

1. ʔaghádit she had a misscarriage / she had an abortion 2. musār (m.) agitated 3. maʔulyīʃ it was canceled 4. maʔanhítʃ I didn't finish / you (m.) didn't finish / she didn't finish 5. ʔa3ádd he prepared 6. ú3dim he was executed 7. ħatinqízu you (pl.) will save 8. itīħ (m.) permit! 9. mabyisbítʃ he doesn't prove / he isn't proving

4.5.1. 1. itsábbit be(come) stabilized 2. itdárrab be coached 3. itṣaħħaħ be corrected 4. it3áyyid be celebrated 5. itsámma be named

4.5.2. 1. itʔákkid he was certain 2. itgawwízu they got married 3. batkállim I speak 4. lāzim tit3áwwid you (m.) need to get accustomed 5. ħatit3áyyin she'll be appointed 6. itʔaxxártu you (pl.) were late 7. matfarrágtiʃ I didn't watch 8. 3ayzīn nittálla? we want to get divorced 9. matɣaddāʃ he didn't eat lunch 10. líssa mit3aʃʃíyya she just ate dinner

4.5.3. 1. he wants to speak 2. we need to have lunch 3. I learn / I'm learning 4. she doesn't want to watch 5. I / you (m.) ate dinner 6. I / you (m.) / she didn't eat dinner 7. he is certain 8. she got divorced 9. we learned 10. you (pl.) moved 11. he gets ready / he's getting ready 12. they want to get married 13. they just graduated 14. he doesn't get ready / he isn't getting ready 15. it was cleaned 16. you (pl.) won't learn 17. (f.) speak! 18. (m.) speak! / he spoke 19. it is (being) celebrated 20. they weren't appointed

4.5.4. 1. it3allímt 2. it3allímit 3. itɣáddit 4. matɣaddítʃ 5. matɣaddítʃ 6. itɣaddēt 7. itɣaddēt 8. matɣaddítʃ 9. miʃ ħatityádda 10. miʃ ħatitfárrag 11. mabtitfarrágʃ 12. mabyitfarragūʃ 13. biyitfarrágu 14. itfarrágu 15. itfarrágna 16. itsammēna 17. matsammināʃ 18. mabnitsammāʃ 19. mabyitsammāʃ 20. mabtitsammīʃ

4.6.1. 1. they met each other 2. they didn't meet each other 3. I'm (getting) annoyed 4. she/it was hidden 5. they forgave each other 6. they didn't forgive each other 7. they forgive each other 8. I played sick / you (m.) played sick 9. she played sick 10. I didn't play sick / you (m.) didn't play sick 11. she didn't play sick 12. you (pl.) pretended to be blind 13. it was just answered 14. we'll cope 15. they competed / (pl.) compete! 16. I (f.) don't want to be annoyed 17. they don't meet each other / they aren't meeting each other 18. we need

to forgive each other 19. you (pl.) tease each other / you're teasing each other 20. it (f.) wasn't found

4.7.1. 1. it (m.) was written 2. you (pl.) were forgotten 3. I was born 4. they were damaged 5. he was annoyed 6. it was stolen 7. they were loved 8. he/it was forgotten

4.7.2. 1. it is written 2. he'll be born 3. I want to be loved 4. we get annoyed / we're getting annoyed 5. he intends to get caught 6. it is (being) cooked 7. it's (being) damaged 8. I'll be forgotten

4.7.3. 1. biyitkítib 2. bititnísu 3. batwílid 4. biyitḍárru 5. mabityázʃ 6. mabyitsiríʔʃ 7. biyitħábbu 8. mabyitnisīʃ

4.7.4. 1. mabyitkitíbʃ 2. miʃ ħayitwílid 3. miʃ 3āyiz atħább 4. mabnityázʃ 5. miʃ nāwi yitmísik 6. mabtittibíxʃ 7. mabyitḍárriʃ 8. miʃ ħatnísi

4.7.5. 1. it was written 2. it wasn't written 3. I bowed 4. we got wet 5. it opens / it's opening 6. it is sold / it's being sold 7. it isn't (being) sold 8. he doesn't want to get wet 9. I didn't bow / you (m.) didn't bow 10. you (f.) didn't bow 11. ħatinkítib 12. inbā3 13. ħayinfítiħ 14. biyinḍírib 15. mabyinḍiríbʃ 16. inʃárit 17. bitinħáll 18. lāzim tinbā3 19. inkítmi 20. matinzi3gūʃ

4.8.1. 1. lāzim aftíkir I need to remember, 2. biyiʃtáɣal he's working, 3. bitiħtāg she needs, 4. irtāħu they relaxed, 5. biyihtámmu they are interested, 6. iʃtarētu you (pl.) bought 7. intáha it (m.) ended, 8. 3ayzīn yiħtállu they want to occupy, 9. líssa mibtidi it just began, 10. ħatixtāri you (f.) will choose, 11. iħtírmu (pl.) respect!, 12. iħtírim(m.) respect!, 13. iktaʃáfna we discovered, 14. mabtintiqidʃ she doesn't complain, 15. maxtaláfʃ it didn't differ, 16. líssa mistilfīn they just borrowed, 17. ittáħadit it (f.) united, 18. matintiqdīʃ (f.) don't criticize, 19. maqtaraħūʃ they didn't suggest, 20. bitistílmu you (pl.) receive

4.8.2. 1. i and t 2. a 3. i 4. iʃtáɣal 5. yiʃtáɣal

4.8.3. 1. I don't remember 2. I'll work 3. you (m.) need / she needs 4. I relaxed / you (m.) relaxed 5. they received 6. it ended 7. it didn't end 8. I don't want to buy 9. (f.) be interested 10. they discovered 11. ibtáda 12. mabtadāʃ 13. mattaħádʃ 14. baxtār 15. mabaxtárʃ 16. bitixtilfu 17. ħaniqtíriħ 18. mabyintiqídʃ 19. mixtār 20. mixtār

4.8.5. 1. uħtúrim 2. uxtīru 3. ħatuʃtára 4. maħtúlliʃ 5. uktúffit 6. uṣṭádu 7. maqturíħʃ 8. bantaqad

4.8.6. 1. ħayuħtáram he will be respected 2. uħtúllit it (f.) was occupied 3. ustúlim it (m.) was received 4. untúxibu they were elected 5. mabyustalámʃ it (m.) isn't (being) received 6. lāzim tuxtáṣar it (f.) needs to be summarized

4.9.1. 1. you (f.) turned red / you got sunburned 2. he's going bald 3. it didn't turn green 4. I/you (m.)/she didn't lose an eye 5. we want to suntan 6. it'll turn white

4.9.2. 1. bitibyị́ḍ̣ 2. biyiwḥíʃʃ 3. biyizríʔʔ 4. baḥwíll 5. biniṣlí33 6. biyismírru

4.9.3. 1. mabtibyíḍḍiʃ it doesn't turn white / it isn't turning white 2. mabyiwḥíʃʃiʃ he isn't becoming ugly 3. mabyizríʔʔiʃ it doesn't turn blue / it isn't turning blue 4. mabaḥwílliʃ I'm not becoming cross-eyed 5. mabniṣlí33iʃ we aren't going bald 6. mabyismirrúʃ they don't suntan / they aren't suntanning

4.10.1. 1. she used 2. she didn't use 3. I used / you (m.) used 4. you (f.) used 5. he uses 6. he doesn't use / he isn't using 7. I'll use 8. you (m.) want to use 9. they don't use / they aren't using 10. they used / (pl.) use! 11. he isn't willing to tolerate 12. they just used 13. we need to hurry 14. he considered pleasant 15. you (pl.) enjoy / you're enjoying 16. I didn't economize / you (m.) didn't economize 17. you (f.) will be surprised 18. I don't enjoy / I'm not enjoying 19. you mustn't hurry 20. 3áli doesn't use / 3áli isn't using

4.10.2. 1. he resigned 2. they benefited 3. I want to respond 4. we resign / we're resigning 5. you (m.) don't respond / you're not responding / she doesn't respond / she isn't responding 6. you (f.) mustn't underestimate 7. you (pl.) will benefit 8. he underestimated

4.10.3. 1. I felt warm 2. she had her fill 3. they provoked 4. they don't provoke / they aren't provoking 5. it/he'll continue 6. you (f.) deserved 7. he finds enjoyable 8. I don't find enjoyable

4.11.1. 1. mastiʔakkídʃ he wasn't certain 2. mastilaʔʔáfʃ he didn't catch 3. mastirayyaḥítʃ she didn't relax 4. mastaḥammúʃ they didn't bathe 5. mastalaʔʔáʃ he didn't receive 6. mastannítʃ she didn't wait 7. mastibarkúʃ they didn't receive blessings 8. mastaḥíltiʃ I/you (m.) didn't deserve

4.11.2. 1. biyistiʔákkid 2. biyistiláʔʔaf 3. bitistiráyyaḥ 4. biyistaḥámmu 5. biyistaláʔʔa 6. bitistánna 7. biyistibárku 8. bastāhil / bitistāhil

4.12.1. 1. he chatted 2. she braked 3. I tripped / you (m.) tripped 4. they translated 5. it rolled 6. they electrocuted 7. you (f.) confused 8. we controlled

4.12.2. 1. madardíʃʃ 2. mafarmilítʃ 3. maʃankíltiʃ 4. matargimúʃ 5. madaḥrágʃ 6. makahrabúʃ 7. malaxbaṭíʃ 8. masayṭarnáʃ

4.12.3. 1. biydárdiʃ 2. bitfármil 3. baʃánkil / bitʃánkil 4. biytargímu 5. biydáḥrag 6. biykahrábu 7. bitlaxbáṭi 8. binsáyṭar

4.12.4. 1. mabyidardíʃʃ 2. mabitfarmílʃ 3. mabaʃankílʃ / mabitʃankílʃ 4. mabyitargimúʃ 5. mabyidaḥrágʃ 6. mabyikahrabúʃ 7. mabitlaxbaṭíʃ 8. mabinsayṭárʃ

4.12.5. 1. targímt 2. matargímtiʃ 3. matargimítʃ 4. miʃ ḥattárgim 5. miʃ ḥaytárgim 6. miʃ ḥaysáyṭar 7. mabyisayṭárʃ 8. biysáyṭar 9. bitsayṭáru 10. sayṭáru 11. matsayṭarúʃ 12.

matfarmilúʃ 13. mabitfarmilúʃ 14. bitfarmílu 15. biyfarmílu 16. farmílu 17. mifarmilīn 18. mifarmíla 19. milaxbáṭa 20. tiláxbaṭ

4.12.6. 1. I tripped 2. it was translated 3. it wasn't translated 4. we got angry 5. you (m.) will be electrocuted 6. (m.) don't slip! 7. I'm worried 8. you (pl.) aren't getting angry

4.12.7. 1. she felt reassured 2. maṭmaʔannítʃ 3. I feel reassured 4. ḥatiṭmaʔánn 5. iṭmaʔánnu 6. I want to feel reassured 7. mabniṭmaʔánniʃ 8. I felt reassured

4.13.1. 1. I came / you (m.) came 2. he came 3. she came 4. they came 5. I come 6. you (m./f.) come / she comes 7. he'll come 8. I (f.) want to come

4.13.2. 1. magítʃ 2. magáʃ 3. magátʃ 4. magūʃ 5. mabagíʃ 6. mabitgíʃ 7. miʃ ḥayīgi 8. miʃ áyz- āgi

4.13.3. 1. magnáʃ 2. biyīgi 3. húwwa gayy 4. húmma miʃ gayyīn 5. mabitgúʃ 6. híyya gáyya 7. ta3āla 8. matgíʃ

4.13.4. 1. he gave 2. they gave / (pl.) give! 3. he gives / he's giving 4. you (m./f.) give / you're giving / she gives / she's giving 5. they'll give 6. (m./f.) give! 7. (f.) giving 8. I (m.) want to give

4.13.5. 1. maddáʃ 2. maddūʃ 3. mabyiddíʃ 4. mabtiddíʃ 5. miʃ ḥayíddu 6. matiddíʃ 7. miʃ middíyya 8. miʃ 3áyiz áddi

4.13.6. 1. maddināʃ 2. 3aʃān maddíʃ 3. ḥatíddu 4. íddu 5. bitíddi 6. bitíddi 7. maddítʃ 8. míddi

4.13.7. 1. I ate / you (m.) ate 2. (pl.) eat! 3. they didn't eat 4. I ate / I'm eating 5. he eats / he's eating 6. he doesn't eat / he isn't eating 7. you (m.) will eat / she'll eat 8. you (f.) will eat

4.13.8. 1. xadt I took 2. xádu they took 3. maxadūʃ they didn't take 4. bāxud I take / I'm taking 5. biyāxud he takes / he's taking 6. mabyaxúdʃ he doesn't take / he isn't taking 7. ḥatāxud you (m.) will take, she'll take 8. ḥatáxdi you (f.) will take

4.13.9. 1. binākul 2. kúl 3. bitáklu 4. mabyaklúʃ 5. maxádʃ 6. xádit 7. mataxúdʃ 8. 3āyiz yāxul 9. húwwa líssa wākil 10. mittáxda

4.13.10. 1. it was eaten 2. you (m.) are (being) taken / it's (being) taken 3. it needs to be eaten 4. they'll be taken 5. mabyittaxídʃ 6. ittaxídt 7. ḥatittáxdu 8. mattaxdítʃ

4.13.11. 1. she found 2. you (m./f.) find / you're finding / she finds / she's finding 3. I (m.) want to find 4. he'll find 5. he didn't find 6. lāʔu 7. binlāʔi 8. lāzim matlaʔúʃ 9. húwwa líssa lāʔi 10. málʔi

4.13.12. 1. I stood 2. I (m.) am standing 3. I stand 4. they fell 5. they didn't stand 6. wiʔi3 7. híyya wáʔfa 8. wáʔfu 9. biyúʔa3 10. mabyuʔáfʃ

4.13.13. *1. he called to prayer 2. he didn't call to prayer 3. they need to call to prayer 4. I'll call to prayer 5. húwwa líssa míddan 6. biníddan 7. 3áyza tíddan 8. matiddánʃ*

4.13.14. *1. c. 2. b. 3. a. 4. a. 5. c. 6. b.*

4.14.1. *1. biyxámmin 2. biyitgāwib 3. biyzākir 4. biytī̄ʃ 5. biydárdiʃ 6. biyistá3mil 7. biyinbáll 8. biyixtílif*

4.14.2. *1. mabiyxammínʃ 2. mabyitgawíbʃ 3. mabiyzakírʃ 4. mabiytī̄ʃ 5. mabiydardíʃʃ 6. mabyista3mílʃ 7. mabyinbálliʃ 8. mabyixtilíʃʃ*

4.14.3. *1. xammínit 2. itgáwbit 3. zákrit 4. ʔatā̄hit 5. dardíʃit 6. ista3mílit 7. inbállit 8. ixtálafit*

4.14.4. *1. ihtámmit 2. bititḥább 3. binixtār 4. biyyánnu 5. ʔabílt 6. masafírtiʃ 7. wárrit 8. magítʃ 9. matitnarfizīʃ 10. mawiʔ3uʃ 11. ḥatitxárrag 12. itdayíʔt 13. ismárru 14. 3áyza - t3állim 15. ta3ālu 16. matgūʃ*

5.1.1. *1. he thanked me 2. he saw us 3. he thanked you (m.) 4. you saw you (f.) 5. he thanked you (pl.) 6. he thanked him 7. he saw her 8. he thanked them*

5.1.2. *1. ʃakarítni 2. ʃafítna 3. ʃakarítak 4. ʃafítik 5. ʃakarítku 6. ʃakarítu 7. ʃafítha 8. ʃakaríthum*

5.1.3. *1. ʃakarūni 2. ʃafūna 3. ʃakarūk 4. ʃafūki 5. ʃakarūku 6. ʃakarū 7. ʃafūha 8. ʃakarūhum*

5.1.4. *1. ʃakartíni 2. ʃuftína 3. ʃakártak 4. ʃúftik 5. ʃakartúku 6. ʃakártu 7. ʃuftáha 8. ʃakartúhum*

5.1.5. *1. you (m.) thanked me 2. you (m.) saw us 3. I thanked you (m.) 4. I saw you (f.) 5. I thanked you (pl.) 6. I thanked him / you (m.) thanked him 7. I saw her / you (m.) saw her 8. I thanked them / you (m.) thanked them*

5.1.6. *1. maʃakaritnīʃ 2. maʃafitnāʃ 3. maʃakaritákʃ 4. maʃafitkīʃ 5. maʃakaritkūʃ 6. maʃakaritūʃ 7. maʃafithāʃ 8. maʃakarithúmʃ*

5.1.7. *1. maʃakarunīʃ 2. maʃafunāʃ 3. maʃakarúkʃ 4. maʃafukīʃ 5. maʃakarukūʃ 6. maʃakaruhūʃ 7. maʃafuhāʃ 8. maʃakaruhúmʃ*

5.1.8. *1. maʃakartinīʃ 2. maʃuftināʃ 3. maʃakartákʃ 4. maʃuftikīʃ 5. maʃakartukūʃ 6. maʃakartūʃ 7. maʃuftahāʃ 8. maʃakartuhúmʃ*

5.1.9. *1. kátabu he wrote it 2. baktíbu I write it / I'm writing it 3. makasarítuʃ she didn't break it 4. bitḥíbbu she loves him 5. 3āyiz azúru I want to visit him 6. banū they built it 7. iʃtarā he bought it 8. makalnahúʃ*

5.1.10. *1. katábha 2. baktíbha 3. makasarithāʃ 4. bitḥibbáha 5. 3āyiz azúrha 6. banūha 7. iʃtaráha 8. makalnahāʃ*

5.1.11. *1. maʃafunīʃ 2. mawwitítu 3. ḥatdarrábhum 4. ḥarraknāha 5. baḥtirímik 6. mabaḥtirmūʃ 7. fatáḥtu 8.*

madarasuhūʃ 9. láḥamik 10. mabyifhamunīʃ 11. simí3tak 12. masmi3tákʃ 13. 3āyiz albísu 14. iʃtartūha 15. kúlu 16. kulīhu 17. maʔultúʃ 18. miʃ ḥākulu 19. lāzim tib3īha 20. lāzim matbi3ihāʃ 21. ramítha 22. nisītu 23. nasitnā 24. mansinahūʃ 25. baḥuttáha 26. bitkammilū 27. sa3dūni 28. bityannī 29. bityannū 30. maʔabiltuhúmʃ 31. húwwa líssa wáklu 32. híyya líssa mwarriyyāha 33. biyixtarūni 34. ʃankiltīni 35. biydaḥrágha 36. húmma líssa katbínu 37. mabtiddihūʃ 38. mabtidduhāʃ 39. ḥayistannāna 40. biyistaʃwī

5.2.1. *1. He gave me a book. 2. You (m.) wrote me a letter. 3. I wrote you (m.) a letter. 4. She lent him the car. 5. I told them the news. / You (m.) told them the news. 6. He'll bring you (f.) a present. 7. He'll give you (f.) a present. 8. you (pl.) showed us the letter. (Note: Each of the sentences can also be translated using 'to' in English, for example, He gave a book to me.)*

5.2.2. *1. maddalīʃ kitāb. 2. makatabtilīʃ gawāb. 3. makatabtilákʃ gawāb. 4. masallifitlūʃ il3arabíyya. 5. maʔultilhúmʃ ilxábar. 6. miʃ ḥaygíblik hidíyya. 7. miʃ ḥayiddālik hidíyya. 8. mawarritulnāʃ ilgawāb.*

5.2.3. *1. biyiddíli kitāb. 2. bitiktíbli gawāb. 3. baktíblak gawāb. 4. bitsallíflu -l3arabíyya. 5. baʔúlhum ilxábar. / bitʔúlhum ilxábar. 6. biygíblik hidíyya. 7. biyiddālik hidíyya. 8. bitwarrúlna -lgawāb.*

5.2.4. *1. mabyiddilīʃ kitāb. 2. mabtiktiblīʃ gawāb. 3. mabaktiblákʃ gawāb. 4. mabitsalliflūʃ il3arabíyya. 5. mabaʔulhúmʃ ilxábar. / mabitʔulhúmʃ ilxábar. 6. mabiygiblíkʃ hidíyya. 7. mabyiddalíkʃ hidíyya. 8. mabitwarrulnāʃ ilgawāb.*

5.2.5. *1. katabítli gawāb. 2. biyʔúlli ʔíṣṣa. 3. iddúlna kitāb. 4. iddílhum kitāb. 5. bitnawílli gawāb. 6. sallifúli -lkitāb. 7. ḥagiblúku hidíyya. 8. mamallalīʃ ilʔíṣṣa. 9. makatabulkīʃ. 10. binwarrílhum il3arabíyya. 11. masallimtilīʃ ilgawāb. 12. lāzim tinawílha -lgawāb. 13. 3ayzīn yib3atúlku -lgawāb. 14. ḥaʔullúhum ilxábar. 15. maʔultilhúmʃ ilxábar. 16. mabiyʔullahāʃ ʔíṣṣa. 17. ib3átlu gawāb. 18. gibtílha hiddíyya. 19. nawiltílna -l3arabíyya. 20. matiddilhāʃ il3arabíyya.*

5.3.1. *1. He gave it to me. / He gave me it. 2. You (m.) wrote it to me. 3. I wrote it to you (m.). 4. She lent it to me. 5. I told it to them. 6. He'll bring you (f.) it. 7. He'll give you (f.) it. 8. You (pl.) showed it to us.*

5.3.2. *1. katabithúli. 2. biyʔulhāli. 3. idduhúlna. 4. iddihulhum. 5. bitnawilhúli. 6. sallifuhúli. 7. ḥagibhálku. 8. mamallahalīʃ. 9. makatabulkīʃ. 10. binwarrihálhum. 11. masallimtihulīʃ. 12. lāzim tinawilhúha. 13. 3ayzīn yib3atuhúlku. 14. ḥaʔulhúlhum. 15. maʔultuhulhúmʃ. 16. mabiyʔulhalāʃ. 17. ib3áthúlu. 18. gibtahálha. 19. nawiltahálna. 20. matiddihalhāʃ.*

6.1.1. *1. Sámya's a student. 2. I (m.) am hungry. 3. The book's on the table. 4. He's at the doctor's. 5. The present's in the car. 6. ḥussām and Xālid are in Egypt. 7. Dīna's beautiful. 8. We're at school.*

6.1.2. 1. sámya miʃ ṭálba. 2. ána miʃ ga3ān. 3. ikkitāb miʃ fōʔ ittarabēza. 4. húwwa miʃ 3and idduktūr. 5. ilhidíyya miʃ fi -l3arabíyya. 6. ḥussām wi xālid miʃ fī maṣr. 7. dīna miʃ gamīla. 8. íḥna miʃ fi -lmadrása.

6.1.3. 1. 1. sámya kānit ṭálba. 2. kúntə ga3ān (Note: The vowel ə is inserted to avoid three adjacent consonants.) 3. ikkitāb kān fōʔ ittarabēza. 4. kān 3and idduktūr. 5. ilhidíyya kānit fi -l3arabíyya. 6. ḥussām wi xālid kānu fī maṣr. 7. dīna kānit gamīla. 8. íḥna kúnna fi -lmadrása.

6.1.4. 1. 1. sámya makanítʃ ṭálba. 2. makúntiʃ ga3ān 3. ikkitāb makánʃ fōʔ ittarabēza. 4. makánʃ 3and idduktūr. 5. ilhidíyya makanítʃ fi -l3arabíyya. 6. ḥussām wi xālid makanūʃ fī maṣr. 7. dīna makanítʃ gamīla. 8. íḥna makunnāʃ fi -lmadrása.

6.1.5. 1. ḥasan makánʃ hína. 2. húwwa nāwi ykūn fi -lmadrása. 3. ikkitāb fōʔ ittarabēza. 4. ínti ga3āna. 5. íḥna miʃ fī maṣr. 6. makunnāʃ fī maṣr. 7. ilmudárris fi -l3arabíyya. 8. naṣra ḥaykūn 3and idduktūr. 9. húda 3áyza tkūn gamīla. 10. iṭṭālib lāzim maykúnʃ fōʔ ittarabēza. 11. ḥasan miʃ hína. 12. kúntu fi -lmadrása. 13. ikkitāb kān fōʔ ittarabēza. 14. kúnti ga3āna. 15. húmma fī maṣr. 16. húmma kānu fī maṣr. 17. ilmu3allíma hatkūn fi -l3arabíyya. 18. naṣra makánʃ fi -lbēt. 19. nabīl miʃ 3āyiz yikūn fi -l3arabíyya. 20. makuntiʃ hína.

6.1.6. 1. they're doing 2. they aren't doing 3. they were doing 4. they weren't doing 5. they did 6. they didn't do 7. they had done 8. they hadn't done 9. they'll do 10. they won't do 11. they'll be doing. 12. they won't be doing 13. they'll have done 14. they won't have done 15. they were going to do 16. they weren't going to do

6.1.7. 1. babni 2. mababniʃ 3. kúntə bábni 4. makúntiʃ bábni 5. banēt 6. mabanítʃ 7. kúntə banēt 8. makúntiʃ banēt 9. ḥábni 10. miʃ ḥábni 11. ḥakūn bábni 12. miʃ ḥakūn bábni 13. ḥakūn banēt 14. miʃ ḥakūn banēt 15. kúntə ḥábni 16. makúntiʃ ḥábni
6.1.8. 1. kúntə batfárrag 2. miʃ ḥakūn ʔanhēt/intahēt 3. kúnna ḥanrūḥ 4. ḥatkūn bitfárrag 5. kúnti ʔanhēti/intah ēti 6. kúntu

ʃúftu 7. makúntūʃ ʃúftu 8. ḥaykūn kal 9. kān ḥayākul 10. ḥatkūn bitúskun

6.1.9. 1. he was going 2. she was coming 3. I (f.) will be standing 4. you (pl.) will be going 5. I (m.) wasn't sitting / you (m.) weren't sitting 6. makánʃ wāʔif 7. ḥatkunu gayyīn 8. íḥna rayḥīn 9. makanítʃ ráyḥa 10. ḥaykūnu ʔa3dīn

6.2.1. 1. I have 2. he doesn't have 3. we have 4. I have 5. he doesn't have 6. we don't have 7. you (m.) have 8. she has

6.2.2. 1. I have a car. 2. She has a headache. 3. We have a brother. 4. He has a sister. 5. I have a lighter (on me). 6. He has money (on him). 7. They have a beautiful house. 8. He has friends.

6.2.3. 1. ma3andīʃ 3arabíyya. 2. ma3andahāʃ ṣudā3. 3. malnāʃ axx. 4. malūʃ uxt. 5. mam3īʃ wallā3a. 6. mam3ahūʃ filūs 7. ma3anduhúmʃ bēt gamīl. 8. malūʃ aṣḥāb.

6.2.4. 1. I had a big book. 2. Rīm had a headache. 3. The house will have a big room. 4. The student want to have a car. 5. You (f.) had a letter (with you). 6. We had water (with us). 7. Sa3īd has a brother and a sister. 8. The teacher (m.) will have a beautiful (nice) room in the school.

6.2.5. 1. makánʃə 3ándi kitāb. 2. rīm makánʃə 3andáha ṣudā3. 3. ilbēt miʃ ḥaykūn lu ʔōḍa kbīra. 4. iṭṭālib miʃ 3āyiz yikūn 3ándu 3arabíyya. 5. makánʃə ma3āki gawāb. 6. makánʃə ma3āna máyya. 7. sa3īd malūʃ ax walla uxt. 8. ilmudárris miʃ ḥaykūn 3ándu ʔōḍa gamīla fi -lmadrása.

6.2.6. 1. 3amrə malūʃ aṣḥāb. 2. idduktūr kān 3ándu bēt kibīr. 3. mam3īʃ ʔakl. 4. ma3andahāʃ ʃánṭa gamīla. 5. fawzíyya malhāʃ axx. 6. līki/líki 3inēn gamīla 7. 3úmar 3ándu kām sána? 8. ána 3āyiz yikūn 3ándi ʔōḍa kbīra. 9. makánʃ 3andína 3arabíyya. 10. mágdi 3ándu húmma.

7.

	sound	hollow	defective	geminate
measure I	ḥílim *dream* kátab *write* ʃáraḥ *explain*	ʔāl *say* gāb *bring* kān *be* nām *sleep* ṭār *fly* xāf *be afraid*	báʔa *become* gíri *run* nísi *forget* ráma *throw*	baṣṣ *look* ḥabb *love*
measure II	náḍḍaf *clean* 3állim *teach*		ɣánna *sing*	
measure III	ḥāwil *try* sā3id *help*			
measure IV	ʔá3lan *announce*	ʔatāḥ *allow*	ʔálɣa *cancel*	ʔa3ádd *prepare*
measure V	it3áwwid *get used to (it)*			
measure VI	itnākif *tease each other*			
measure VII	itwálad *be born*	inbā3 *be sold* itbā3 *be sold*	itnása *be forgotten*	inbáll *get wet*
measure VIII	istálaf *borrow*	ixtār *choose*	iʃtára *buy*	ihtámm *be interested*
measure IX	iṣlá33 *go bald*			
measure X	istámta3 *enjoy* (irregular) istánna *wait*	istafād *benefit*	istádfa *feel warm*	istaḥáʔʔ *deserve* istamárr *continue*
measure X+II			istaḥámma *bathe*	
measure X + III				
measure XI	dárdiʃ *chat*			
measure XI passive	itzáḥlaʔ			
irregular	gih *come* ídda *give* xad *take*			

7.1.1. 1. ʃaráḥt 2. ḥílmit 3. manaḍḍáʃʃ 4. 3allímna 5. kátabu 6. sa3ídti 7. maḥawíltiʃ 8. ʔa3lántu 9. mat3awwídʃ 10. itnákfu 11. itwaládt 12. mastaláftiʃ 13. iṣla33ēt 14. istamtá3na 15. istannēti 16. madardiʃūʃ 17. itzáḥlaʔ 18. maddítiʃ 19. magítʃ 20. maxadnāʃ

7.1.2. 1. ʔúltu 2. makúntiʃ 3. gíbna 4. ṭāru 5. manamítʃ 6. maxáʃʃ 7. ʔatāḥt 8. itbā3it/inbā3it 9. ixtártu 10. mastafadnāʃ 11. maʔalítʃ 12. kānu 13. magibtíʃ 14. maṭírtiʃ 15. nimt 16. xúfna 17. maʔataḥūʃ 18. matbā3iʃ/ manbā3iʃ 19. maxtártiʃ 20. istafádti

7.1.3. 1. baʔēt 2. maramítʃ 3. nísyit 4. magiryūʃ 5. ɣánna 6. ʔálɣēna 7. maʃtartūʃ 8. istadfēt 9. istaḥammēti 10. matnasítʃ 11. mabaʔāʃ 12. maramūʃ 13. manisyūʃ 14. girīt 15. maɣannāʃ 16. maʔalɣitīʃ 17. iʃtárit 18. mastadfítʃ 19. mastaḥammūʃ 20. itnása

7.1.4. 1. baṣṣēt 2. ḥabbēna 3. ʔa3addēt 4. manballitíʃ 5. ihtammētu 6. mastamárriʃ 7. istaḥáʔʔit 8. mabaṣṣināʃ 9. ḥabbēt 10. maʔa3addināʃ 11. inballēt 12. mahtámmiʃ 13. istamarrēti 14. mastaḥáʔʔiʃ

7.1.5. 1. mastamta3ūʃ 2. magtūʃ 3. maṣlá33iʃ 4. makunnāʃ 5. maʃtarūʃ 6. maxtarítʃ 7. mansítʃ 8. maḥabbiʃ 9. makáltiʃ 10. maɣannūʃ 11. madardiʃnāʃ 12. magūʃ 13. magāʃ 14. maramítʃ 15. maramítʃ 16. maramtíʃ 17. maḥlímʃ 18. masa3dūʃ 19. mastamarrítʃ 20. maxuftūʃ

7.1.6. itʃáraħ 2. it3állim 3. itħábbit 4. ʔúʒlinit 5. ʔutīħ 6. itʔāl 7. itsá3dit 8. ittāxid

7.1.7. 1. magrīʃ 2. magiryítʃ 3. gíryit 4. inbállit 5. inballēt 6. inbállu 7. manballúʃ 8. maxadúʃ 9. maxadnāʃ 10. xádna 11. xádtu 12. ʔúltu 13. ʔālu 14. maʔalúʃ 15. maddúʃ 16. madditīʃ 17. maddāʃ 18. ídda 19. ʔálɣa 20. ʔ álɣit

7.1.1. 1. 3āyiz āgi 2. múmkin yíʃli33 3. lāzim ti3línu 4. 3ayzīn yisá3du 5. múmkin tistánni 6. miʃ 3áyza -tzáħlaʔ 7. 3aʃān tāxud 8. 3aʃān manistamtí3ʃ 9. lāzim matiddīʃ 10. miʃ lāzim níʃraħ

7.1.2. 1. 3ayzīn tiʔulu 2. lāzim maykúnʃ 3. miʃ 3āyiz yixtār 4. 3aʃān manxáfʃ 5. miʃ lāzim tinām 6. 3áyza tnām 7. lāzim agīb 8. múmkin yiṭīru

7.2.3. 1. 3ayzīn yiʃtíru 2. lāzim yitnísi 3. musta3ídd tílyi 4. miʃ lāzim níbʔa 5. nawyīn tínsu6. múmkin tiɣánni 7. lāzim matigrūʃ 8. 3aʃān tista ħamma

7.2.4. 1. 3āyiz abuṣṣ 2. lāzim matinballūʃ 3. náwya -stamírr 4. múmkin yihtámmu 5. miʃ lāzim yi3ídd 6. 3aʃān tistaħáʔʔ

7.2.5. 1. maħlámʃ 2. maytíħʃ 3. matħawilʃ 4. maydardiʃūʃ 5. matħibbīʃ 6. matirmūʃ 7. manistadfāʃ 8. mat3allímʃ

7.2.6. 1. maynaḍḍáfʃ 2. titbā3/tinbā3 3. yitsā3id 4. yutāħ 5. titħább 6. atwílid

7.2.7. 1. miʃ 3āyiz áħlam 2. binħíbb nitnākif 3. biyħíbb yináḍḍaf 4. 3áyza tírmi 5. lāzim yistaħámmu 6. 3áyza tistílif 7. múmkin nidárdiʃ 8. 3áyza -ħāwil 9. 10. musta3iddīn yi3allímu 11. nāwi tīgi

7.3.1. 1. bitāxud 2. biníddi 3. biyistannu 4. biyiʃlá33 5. biyit3awwídu 6. bāgi 7. bitíktib 8. mabyiddīʃ 9. bití3lin 10. maba3línʃ 11. mabnaxúdʃ 12. biydardíʃu 13. bititzaħláʔi 14. mabtistamtí3ʃ 15. mabtistanna 16. bastílif 17. biyiʃráħu 18. mabtiʃraħūʃ 19. mabyinaḍḍáfʃ 20. mabtiħlámʃ

7.3.2. 1. bitistafīdu 2. biyixtarūʃ 3. mabitxáffʃ 4. baṭīr 5. binnām 6. mabitʔulūʃ 7. biygīb 8. biytīħu 9. mabyitbá3ʃ/mabyinbá3ʃ 10. baʔūl 11. mabastafídʃ 12. bitixtāri 13. binxāf 14. mabiyṭírʃ 15. mabiynamūʃ 16. biyʔūlu 17. mabitgíbʃ 18. mabtitħīʃ 19. bititbā3/bitinbā3 20. baxāf

7.3.3. 1. baʃtíri 2. mabnirmīʃ 3. mabtitnisīʃ 4. mabtinsīʃ 5. bitíɣlu 6. biyɣánni 7. bitírmi 8. biyíbʔu 9. biyistaħámma 10. bitistadfāʃ 11. mabniʃtirīʃ 12. bitíɣri 13. biyitnísi 14. binínsa 15. mabalɣīʃ 16. mabitɣannūʃ 17. mabtirmīʃ 18. mabtibʔīʃ 19. mabyistaħammūʃ 20. bastádfa

7.3.4. 1. biybúṣṣ 2. bitihtámm 3. ba3ídd 4. bitħíbbi 5. bitistamírru 6. biyinbáll 7. bitistaħáʔʔi 8. mababúṣṣiʃ 9. mabyihtammūʃ 10. mabit3íddiʃ 11. mabiyħibbūʃ 12. mabtistamírriʃ 13. mabaħíbbiʃ 14. mabnistaħáʔʔiʃ

7.3.5. 1. mabyidríʃ 2. mabiysafrūʃ 3. mabnisarráħʃ 4. mabitxúʃʃiʃ 5. mabiyzúrʃ 6. mabyibdúʃ 7. mabtib3īʃ 8. mabiygīʃ 9. mabastiʔakkídʃ 10. mabtakúlʃ 11. mabtinamúʃ 12. mabitgibūʃ 13. mabyiʃrabūʃ 14. mabyimʃīʃ 15. mabtistirayyaħīʃ 16. mabnityázʃ 17. mabiylaʔīʃ 18. mabitʂaħħáħʃ 19. mabiywarríʃ 20. mabit3abbarīʃ

7.3.6. 1. mabiy3allímʃ 2. biytāħ 3. biyitkítib/biyinkítib 4. bititnísi 5. bituxtār 6. mabtuʃtarāʃ 7. mabtustaxdámʃ 8. biyittākil

7.3.7. 1. banbáll 2. mabitsa3dúʃ 3. biyʔūlu 4. mabyixtárʃ 5. mabnihtámmiʃ 6. mabitħibbūʃ 7. biyɣánni 8. mabiyɣannīʃ 9. bitínsa 10. biy3allímu 11. bitbúṣṣ 12. bitdardíʃu 13. biyíbʔa 14. mabniṭírʃ

7.4.1. 1. ħayíʃraħ 2. ħatāxud 3. ħastánna 4. ħayīgu 5. ħatħáwli 6. miʃ ħayiʂlá33 7. miʃ ħatitzáħlaʔ 8. ħaníħlam 9. ħati3línu 10. miʃ ħáddi

7.4.2. 1. ħaygīb 2. ħayistafīdu 3. ħantīħ 4. miʃ ħaʔūl 5. ħatkūn 6. ħayinbā3/ħatinbā3 7. miʃ ħatxáfi 8. miʃ ħatixtār

7.4.3. 1. miʃ ħatíbʔa 2. ħaniʃtíri 3. ħayyánnu 4. miʃ ħanílyi 5. miʃ ħágri 6. ħatírmi 7. ħánsa 8. ħatistádfu 9. ħatnísi 10. miʃ ħayistaħámma

7.4.4. 1. ħatħíbbu 2. miʃ ħanistamírr 3. ħa3ídd 4. ħaybúṣṣu 5. ħayistaħáʔʔ 6. miʃ ħatihtámm

7.4.5. 1. miʃ ħagīb 2. miʃ ħayiktíbu 3. miʃ ħanistánna 4. miʃ ħatyínni

7.4.6. 1. miʃ ħatíʃraħ 2. ħanīgi 3. ħatínsu 4. miʃ ħaxāf 5. ħayistamírr 6. ħatbúṣṣi 7. miʃ ħatkūnu 8. ħaydárdiʃ 9. ħat3ídd 10. miʃ ħayáklu

7.5.1. 1. uskútu 2. matistilífʃ 3. ta3āli 4. xud 5. matitzaħlaʔúʃ 6. matiʃraħīʃ 7. íḍrab 8. sá3di 9. iktíbi 10. matdardiʃūʃ

7.5.2. 1. nām 2. ixtāri 3. kūnu 4. gīb/hāt 5. matkunīʃ 6. matxafūʃ

7.5.3. 1. íɣri 2. íbʔa 3. íbʔi 4. istaħámmu 5. matinsāʃ 6. matɣannūʃ

7.5.4. 1. matbúṣṣiʃ 2. ihtámmi 3. ħíbbu 4. matistamirrūʃ 5. matinballīʃ 6. i3ídd

7.5.5. 1. matgīʃ 2. matgibūʃ 3. matiktibīʃ 4. matʔabílʃ 5. matʔulūʃ 6. matigrīʃ

7.6.1. 1. ʃāriħ 2. xárga 3. waldīn 4. bāyis 5. rámya 6. ɣannīn 7. midárris/mi3állim 8. miwarríyya 9. miʔablīn 10. mú3lin 11. gáyya 12. waxdīn

7.6.2. *1. Do you (m.) remember me? 2. I (f.) remember you (m.). 3. I (m.) remember you (f.). 4. Do you (pl.) remember us? 5. I (m.) don't remember him. 6. I (f.) don't remember him.*

7.6.3. *1. ínta fakírna? 2. ána miʃ fakírha. 3. ána miʃ fakráha. 4. húmma fakrīnu. 5. húmma fakrínha. 6. híyya fakrāku.*

Appendixes

Appendix A: Common Egyptian Names

The following names are used in exercises throughout the book.

men's names	women's names
áħmad	amīna
hāni	dīna
ħásan	farīda
ħāmid	fáṭma
ħussām	fawzíyya
karīm	húda
mágdi	ħusníyya
maħmūd	márwa
muħámmad	máryam
múṣṭafa	múna
nabīl	nágwa
naṣr	nūra
sa3īd	rīm
sāmi	sálma
sāmiħ	sámya
xālid	sāra
yūsif	yásmin
3áli	zēnab
3amr	3abīr
3úmar	3azīza

Appendix B: Conjugation Drill Grids

The following two pages contain grids to help you practice random conjugation drills. See p. 41 in this book for directions.

Persons and Positive/Negative: Use this grid if you want to practice one certain tense.

húwwa +	húwwa −	híyya +	ínta −	íntu +	íħna −	ínti +	húmma −	íħna +	ínti −	ínta +	ána −
ínti +	íħna +	ínti +	húmma +	íħna +	ána +	híyya −	ána −	íntu −	íħna −	híyya +	húmma −
ínta −	húwwa +	ána −	íntu +	húmma +	húwwa −	íntu −	ínti −	húmma −	ínta +	ána +	íħna +
íħna −	íntu +	íntu −	húwwa +	híyya −	ínta −	ínti +	ána −	húwwa −	ínti −	ínta +	híyya +
ínti −	húmma +	ínta −	íntu +	ána +	húmma −	húwwa +	íħna +	híyya −	ínta +	húwwa −	ínti +
ínta −	íntu −	híyya +	ínta +	híyya −	húwwa +	húmma +	ána −	íħna +	híyya +	íntu +	ána −
húmma −	íntu −	ána −	ínti −	húwwa −	híyya −	ána +	ána −	húwwa +	húmma +	híyya +	ínti +
íntu −	ínta −	íħna +	húwwa −	híyya −	ána −	húmma −	ána +	íħna −	íntu +	ínta +	húmma +
húwwa +	ínti −	húmma −	íntu −	ínti +	íħna +	húmma +	ínta −	híyya +	íntu +	ínta +	íħna −
íħna +	híyya −	íntu −	ínta −	húwwa −	húwwa +	ána −	híyya +	íħna −	ínti +	ínti +	húmma −

Persons and Tense: Use this grid if you want to practice either positive or negative forms of all tenses: perfect, (bare) imperfect, bi-imperfect, and future.

húwwa perfect	húwwa imp.	híyya perfect	ínta bi-imp.	íntu perfect	íħna perfect	ínti bi-imp.	húmma perfect	íħna imp.	ínti perfect	ínta perfect	ána perfect
ínti future	íħna future	ínti bi-imp.	húmma imp.	íħna bi-imp.	ána bi-imp.	híyya future	ána imp.	íntu perfect	íħna bi-imp.	híyya perfect	húmma imp.
ínta bi-imp.	húwwa bi-imp.	ána imp.	íntu future	húmma perfect	húwwa perfect	íntu perfect	ínti bi-imp.	húmma bi-imp.	ínta imp.	ána perfect	íħna bi-imp.
íħna perfect	íntu imp.	íntu perfect	húwwa imp.	híyya bi-imp.	ínta perfect	ínti perfect	ána future	húwwa bi-imp.	ínti perfect	ínta perfect	híyya imp.
ínti bi-imp.	húmma future	ínta perfect	íntu bi-imp.	ána bi-imp.	húmma bi-imp.	húwwa bi-imp.	íħna future	híyya perfect	ínta bi-imp.	húwwa bi-imp.	ínti perfect
ínta future	íntu bi-imp.	híyya bi-imp.	ínta bi-imp.	híyya perfect	húwwa future	húmma perfect	ána perfect	íħna perfect	híyya bi-imp.	íntu bi-imp.	ána future
húmma bi-imp.	íntu bi-imp.	ána perfect	ínti imp.	húwwa future	híyya bi-imp.	ána imp.	ána bi-imp.	húwwa perfect	húmma future	híyya imp.	ínti perfect
íntu imp.	ínta imp.	íħna perfect	húwwa imp.	híyya imp.	ána bi-imp.	húmma bi-imp.	ána bi-imp.	íħna imp.	íntu bi-imp.	ínta imp.	húmma perfect
húwwa perfect	ínti perfect	húmma perfect	íntu perfect	ínti bi-imp.	íħna bi-imp.	húmma imp.	ínta perfect	híyya perfect	íntu perfect	ínta bi-imp.	íħna perfect
íħna imp.	híyya bi-imp.	íntu imp.	ínta bi-imp.	húwwa bi-imp.	húwwa perfect	ána perfect	híyya future	íħna bi-imp.	ínti imp.	ínti imp.	húmma bi-imp.

This page is photocopiable. (www.lingualism.com)

Imperatives: Use this grid if you want to practice positive and negative imperative forms.

ínta +	íntu +	ínti +	ínta -	íntu +	ínti -
ínti -	ínta +	íntu +	ínti -	ínta -	ínti +
íntu +	íntu -	ínta +	ínta -	ínti +	ínta +
íntu -	ínta -	ínti +	ínta +	ínti -	íntu -
íntu +	íntu +	ínta -	ínta +	ínti -	ínti +
íntu -	ínti +	ínti -	ínta -	ínta +	ínta +
ínti -	íntu -	ínti +	ínta -	íntu +	íntu -
íntu +	ínta -	ínti -	ínta +	íntu -	íntu -
íntu -	íntu +	ínta -	ínti -	ínti +	ínta +
ínta -	íntu -	ínta +	ínti +	ínti -	íntu +

Participles: Use this grid to practice the active and passive participles. Note that intransitive verbs (i.e. verbs which no not take an object) generally do not have passive participle forms.

passive masc.	passive plural	passive masc.	active fem.	passive masc.	active masc.	active fem.	passive masc.	active plural	active masc.	active masc.	active masc.
active plural	active plural	active fem.	passive plural	active fem.	active fem.	passive plural	active plural	passive masc.	active fem.	passive masc.	passive plural
active fem.	passive fem.	active plural	passive plural	passive masc.	passive masc.	passive masc.	active fem.	passive fem.	active plural	active masc.	active fem.
active masc.	passive plural	passive masc.	passive plural	passive fem.	active masc.	active masc.	active plural	passive fem.	active masc.	active masc.	passive plural
active fem.	passive plural	active masc.	passive fem.	active fem.	passive fem.	passive fem.	active plural	passive masc.	active fem.	passive fem.	active masc.
active plural	passive fem.	passive fem.	active fem.	passive masc.	passive plural	passive masc.	active masc.	active masc.	passive fem.	passive fem.	active plural
passive fem.	passive fem.	active masc.	active plural	passive plural	passive fem.	active plural	active fem.	passive masc.	passive plural	passive plural	active masc.
passive plural	active plural	active masc.	passive plural	passive plural	active fem.	passive fem.	active fem.	active plural	passive fem.	active plural	passive masc.
passive masc.	active masc.	passive masc.	passive masc.	active fem.	active fem.	passive plural	active masc.	passive masc.	passive masc.	active fem.	active masc.
active plural	passive fem.	passive plural	active fem.	passive fem.	passive masc.	active masc.	passive plural	active fem.	active plural	active plural	passive fem.

This page is photocopiable. (www.lingualism.com)

Appendix C: Blank Conjugation Table

	positive	negative	
ána			**perfect**
íḥna			
ínta			
ínti			
íntu			
húwwa			
híyya			
húmma			

	positive	negative	
ána			**imperfect**
íḥna			
ínta			
ínti			
íntu			
húwwa			
híyya			
húmma			

	positive	negative	
ána			**bi-imperfect**
íḥna			
ínta			
ínti			
íntu			
húwwa			
híyya			
húmma			

	positive	negative	
ána			**future**
íḥna			
ínta			
ínti			
íntu			
húwwa			
híyya			
húmma			

	positive	negative	
ínta			**imperative**
ínti			
íntu			

	active	passive	
masculine			**participles**
feminine			
plural			

This page is photocopiable. (www.lingualism.com)

Appendix D: Cards of Verbs from Verb Tables

ḍárab yíḍrab	kátab yíktib	ṭálab yúṭlub
ʃírib yíʃrab	mísik yímsik	síkin yúskun
	ʔāl yiʔūl	gāb yigīb
nām yinām	xāf yixāf	mála yímla
ráma yírmi	rága yárgu	nísi yínsa
míʃi yímʃi	ṣaḥḥ yiṣáḥḥ	ḥaṭṭ yiḥúṭṭ

1s3

sound measure I

request

1s2

sound measure I

write

1s1

sound measure I

hit

1s6

sound measure I

reside, live

1s5

sound measure I

catch, hold

1s4

sound measure I

drink

1h2

hollow measure I

bring

1h1

hollow measure I

say

1d1

defective measure I

fill

1h4

hollow measure I

fear

1h3

hollow measure I

sleep

1d4

defective measure I

forget

1d3

defective measure I

hope for, beg, implore

1d2

defective measure I

throw

1g2

geminate measure I

put

1g1

geminate measure I

be appropriate

1d5

defective measure I

walk

ḥabb yiḥíbb	kámmil yikámmil	fákkar yifákkar
ṭáffa yiṭáffi	Ɂābil yiɁābil	dāwa yidāwi
Ɂáɜlan yíɜlin	Ɂatāḥ yitīḥ	Ɂánha, yínhi
Ɂaɜádd yiɜídd	itɜállim yitɜállim	itḥárrak yitḥárrak
ityādda yityádda	itsābiɁ yitsābiɁ	itɜāma yitɜāma
itmásak yitmísik	inkátam yinkítim	ityāz yityāz

2s2 sound measure II think	**2s1** sound measure II complete	**1g3** geminate measure I love
3d defective measure III cure	**3s** sound measure III meet	**2d** defective measure II extinguish
4d defective measure IV finish	**4h** hollow measure IV permit, allow	**4s** sound measure IV announce
5s2 sound measure V move	**5s1** sound measure V learn	**4g** geminate measure IV prepare
6d defective measure VI pretend to be blind	**6s** sound measure VI compete	**5d** defective measure V have lunch
7h1 hollow measure VII become annoyed	**7s2** sound measure VII be quiet	**7s1** sound measure VII get arrested

inbā3 yinbā3	itnása yitnísi	inħána yinħíni
itħább yitħább	inbáll yinbáll	iħtáram yiħtírim
iʃtáɣal yiʃtáɣal	ixtār yixtār	iʃtára yiʃtíri
iħtáll yiħtáll	iħmárr yiħmírr	istáxdim yistáxdim
istálṭaf yistálṭaf	istafād yistafīd	istáɣla yistáɣla
istágra yistágri	istafázz yistafízz	istaħá?? yistaħá??

7d2 defective measure VII bow	**7d1** defective measure VII be forgotten	**7h2** hollow measure VII be sold
8s1 sound measure VIII respect	**7g2** geminate measure VII get wet	**7g1** geminate measure VII be loved
8d defective measure VIII buy	**8h** hollow measure VIII choose	**8s2** sound measure VIII work
10s1 sound measure X use	**9s** sound measure IX turn red	**8g** geminate measure VIII occupy
10d1 defective measure X consider expensive	**10h** hollow measure X benefit	**10s2** sound measure X consider pleasant
10g2 geminate measure X deserve	**10g1** geminate measure X provoke	**10d2** defective measure X dare

istiʔákkid yistiʔákkid	istiráyyaħ yistiráyyaħ	istaláʔʔa yistaláʔʔa
istánna yistánna	istibārik yistibārik	istāhil yistāhil
tárgim yitárgim	láxbaṭ yiláxbaṭ	itʃánkil yitʃánkil
itzáħlaʔ yitzáħlaʔ	iṭmaʔánn yiṭmaʔánn	gih yīgi
ídda yíddi	kal yākul	ittāxid yittāxid
wíʔif yúʔaf	íddan yíddan	3and- li- ma3a-

10.2d defective measure X + II receive	**10.2s2** sound measure X + II relax	**10.2s1** sound measure X + II be certain
10.3i irregular measure X + III be worth	**10.3s** sound measure X + III receive a blessing	**10.2i** irregular measure X + II wait
11p1 passive measure XI trip	**11s2** sound measure XI mix up	**11s1** sound measure XI translate
i1 irregular come	**11i** irregular measure XI feel reassured	**11p2** passive measure XI slip
i4 irregular find	**i3** irregular eat	**i2** irregular give
have	**i6** irregular call to prayer	**i5** irregular stand

Other titles by Lingualism Publishing

- *Egyptian Colloquial Arabic Verbs: Conjugation Tables and Grammar*

- *Arabic Learner's Dictionary*

- *Modern Standard Arabic Verbs*

- *Top 200 Egyptian Colloquial Arabic Verbs*

Visit our website for information on current and upcoming titles,

free excerpts, and language learning resources.

www.lingualism.com

27976475R00061

Made in the USA
Middletown, DE
27 December 2015